Mobile Learning

Mobile Learning

Shaun Wilden

Great Clarendon Street, Oxford, OX2 6DP, United Kingdom

Oxford University Press is a department of the University of Oxford.
It furthers the University's objective of excellence in research, scholarship,
and education by publishing worldwide. Oxford is a registered trade
mark of Oxford University Press in the UK and in certain other countries

© Oxford University Press 2017

The moral rights of the author have been asserted

First published in 2017

2021 2020 2019 2018 2017

10 9 8 7 6 5 4 3 2 1

No unauthorized photocopying

All rights reserved. No part of this publication may be reproduced, stored
in a retrieval system, or transmitted, in any form or by any means, without
the prior permission in writing of Oxford University Press, or as expressly
permitted by law, by licence or under terms agreed with the appropriate
reprographics rights organization. Enquiries concerning reproduction outside
the scope of the above should be sent to the ELT Rights Department, Oxford
University Press, at the address above

You must not circulate this work in any other form and you must impose
this same condition on any acquirer

Links to third party websites are provided by Oxford in good faith and for
information only. Oxford disclaims any responsibility for the materials
contained in any third party website referenced in this work

ISBN: 978 0 19 420039 4

Printed in China

This book is printed on paper from certified and well-managed sources

ACKNOWLEDGEMENTS

Back cover photograph: Oxford University Press building/David Fisher

The author and publisher are grateful to those who have given permission to reproduce the following extracts and adaptations of copyright material: p.24 Diagram from SAMR Model: 'As we may teach: Educational technology from 'theory into practice' by Ruben Puentedura from http://hippasus.com/rrpweblog. Reproduced by permission.

Illustrations by: Oxford Designers and Illustrators pp.33, 35

For Samuel, for keeping me on my toes.

Contents

Introduction – 9

PART 1   IMPLEMENTING MOBILE DEVICES – 11

1   Thinking about going mobile – 12
Why use mobile devices? – 12
Mobile learning and 21st century skills – 14
Getting the classroom ready – 16

2   Getting started – 20
Preparing the way – 20
Acceptable use policies – 20
Staying safe – 22
Using apps – 23

PART 2   TAKING THE FIRST STEPS – 29

3   Take out your devices – 30
Text messaging – 30
Emoji – 33
Games – 36
Audio recording – 36

4   A photo tells a thousand words – 39
Selfies – 39
Combining photos – 40
Adding text – 41
Sharing photos – 42
Bringing coursebooks to life – 43
Making more of photos – 45

5   QR codes: a versatile classroom tool – 47
What is a QR code? – 47
Making and sharing QR codes – 48
Creating your own content – 49
Student QR codes – 52

CONTENTS

6 Audio recording – *56*
    Voice recognition – *56*
    Making recordings – *57*
    Podcasting – *60*

PART 3 MOBILE DEVICES: PROJECTS AND BEYOND – *63*

7 Digital storytelling – *64*
    Why digital storytelling? – *64*
    Planning a digital story – *66*
    Trailers as digital stories – *68*
    Assessing students' digital stories – *69*

8 Video and animation – *72*
    Short-form video – *73*
    Creating longer videos – *74*
    Avatars – *75*
    App smashing – *76*
    Animation – *77*

9 Multimodal approaches and alternative realities – *79*
    Adding links, videos, and text to an image – *79*
    Augmented reality – *81*
    Virtual reality – *85*

10 Tools for the teacher – *88*
    Screen recording – *88*
    Flipped learning – *90*
    Mobile devices and informal assessment – *91*
    Using digital coursebooks – *94*

    Glossary – *97*
    Useful apps and websites – *99*

Introduction

Living in a mobile world

The fact that we live in a mobile world may be yesterday's news, but here are a few statistics about the use of mobile devices that might still surprise and impress you:
- At the time of writing, there are around 7.5 billion mobile phones and tablets in use around the world. In other words, there are more mobile devices on the planet than people.
- Fifty per cent of the world's population owns a mobile device.
- More than 100 countries have more mobile phones in use than the population of that country.
- The number of mobile devices in use is currently growing five times faster than the global population.
- Adults look at their device on average once every six minutes.

As these statistics show, mobile devices are considered a necessity for most of us today. We use them for communication, to view and create media such as photos and videos, and even to settle arguments by quickly searching for the answer on the web. So why are they not used more as part of everyday teaching? And why is it that many educational institutions ban the use of mobile devices?

Meeting the challenges

Despite their potential, mobile devices often pose a dilemma for teachers. On the one hand, we can see how integral they are to everyday life, and recognize that they are powerful multimedia tools which can really enhance our educational toolkit. On the other hand, we are frequently faced with media scare stories about the possible downsides of using mobile devices in education and a general reluctance of educational establishments to allow their use. A quick internet search of newspaper headlines shows that some form of scare story related to mobile technology appears every month – from text language destroying our ability to use 'real' language, to smartphones being a source of distraction in class. There may also be a general weariness towards 'yet another new classroom technology', or perhaps a fear that the device will be more engaging than the lesson itself and become a Pandora's Box of distraction. And although there are around three billion smartphones in use around the world, teachers tend not to have the most cutting edge of devices, which can make us more reluctant to use them with students. This is not helped by the fact that mobile technology is constantly changing. While the functionality of a mobile device may remain fairly fixed, the differences between operating systems and constant upgrades can make them seem all the more unmanageable. For all of these reasons and more, teachers may approach mobile learning somewhat nervously, unsure of what to do and where to begin.

INTRODUCTION

Who this book is for

Many teachers will already be familiar with the term 'e-learning', which refers to the use of electronic devices such as computers and the internet to assist education. Often the learning takes place outside the classroom, with students accessing a language learning program or website. With the increasing use of mobile devices, we are now also using the term 'mobile learning' or 'm-learning': learning through the use of mobile devices. The advantage of mobile learning is that it has the ability to bring real life into the classroom.

Mobile devices open up a whole world of possibilities for teaching. They can be used as a simple means of engagement; or, at the other end of the scale, be used to produce impressive multimedia presentations. Most teachers have turned to technology to enhance their lessons, be it using a cassette recorder, an overhead projector, or a video camera. Typical smartphones and tablets can be everything from a camera to an audio recorder, a word processor, and a video-editing suite. They have easy-to-use operating systems based on touch, gesture, and voice, making them simpler to use than other forms of technology. This book will provide ways of exploiting the simplicity of mobile technology and show you how to approach mobile learning with confidence.

How this book is organized

This book is organized into three parts, with each chapter dealing with a particular aspect of using mobile devices in the classroom. Part 1 addresses their implementation, from planning ahead to thinking about your first lesson. We consider the benefits of mobile learning (Chapter 1) and some of the wider considerations involved (Chapter 2). Part 2 introduces a selection of easy-to-do activities to complement your regular teaching material and build your confidence. We look at some basic features of mobile devices (Chapter 3), plus how to use photos (Chapter 4), QR codes (Chapter 5), and audio recording (Chapter 6). Finally, Part 3 provides ideas for project work (Chapters 7 and 8), considers more complex uses of mobile devices (Chapter 9), and looks at how mobile learning can make life easier for teachers (Chapter 10).

In each chapter, *Try this* activities provide specific ideas that you can try out with your students. *Getting it right* sections offer advice on making the most of specific aspects of mobile learning, and the *Why this works* sections explain the practical rationale for using the tools and techniques recommended. At the back of the book, a *Glossary* is provided for words that appear in bold throughout the main text. This is followed by a *Useful apps and websites* section with links to digital and online resources mentioned in the book.

To get the most out of this book and the suggested activities, try to follow the advice teachers so often give to students: 'practice makes perfect'. When we ask our students to try out new language in speaking or writing, we are asking them to embrace a degree of risk and experimentation. We need to adopt the same approach to mobile learning. Trying new things, experimenting with apps, and using the technology yourself is the best way to gain the confidence and skills required to successfully integrate mobile learning into your lessons. Happy reading, and happy experimenting!

Part 1   Implementing mobile devices

1   Thinking about going mobile

Why use mobile devices?

Whereas computer and laptop use involves pre-planning, whether to book the school's computer room or to ask students to bring their laptops to class, a mobile device is almost always carried by its user. As mobile devices have become ubiquitous among all age groups and across all social boundaries, it is likely that – wherever you are teaching – most students will have some form of mobile device.

What is a mobile device?

The term 'mobile device' refers to a multimedia tool you can put in your pocket and carry around easily, such as a mobile phone, **tablet**, **MP3** player, or an e-reader. **Smartphones** perform many of the functions of a computer, with an operating system that runs **apps** (as opposed to 'basic' mobile phones, which don't usually perform any of these functions). The main differences between smartphones and tablets are that the latter are bigger and can't be used to make calls through a phone network, although it is possible to do so using videoconferencing tools such as Skype or FaceTime. The 'phablet' is a larger type of smartphone which feels more like a small tablet. Another kind of mobile device is 'wearable technology'. This includes activity trackers which can be worn and used to collect information about health and fitness. Smart watches allow users to do some of the things they would normally do with their smartphone, while virtual reality headsets are opening up whole new worlds right before our eyes. For the purposes of this book, 'mobile device' refers specifically to smartphones and tablets.

Breaking down boundaries

Mobile devices as educational tools can help to break down boundaries – in this case, the walls of the classroom. In class, you can exploit the fact that many students will be very familiar with mobile technology and have a strong attachment to their own devices, which they are likely to use on a daily basis to perform a range of functions. For example, students may enjoy taking photos on their device and have a large collection of photos that you can use for tasks and as a stimulus for speaking (with the students' agreement). They may also have specific reasons for choosing their particular device, and you could use this as a means of engagement for a speaking task.

THINKING ABOUT GOING MOBILE

Try this ☞ **Tell me about your device**

Ask students to face each other in two rows. Tell them to talk to the person opposite about their device for one minute, using these prompts:
- Why did you choose that device?
- What do you like about it?
- What would you change?

After one minute, stop them and send the student at the end of one row (not both) to the other end, with the other students in that row moving along to accommodate the change so they all have a new partner. Repeat as many times as you wish. Finally, ask students to discuss how similar their devices are.

✓ **Getting it right** | **Using students' mobile devices**

Ask students to use their own devices for this activity, even if the school plans to provide them, as it's a good way of highlighting the benefits of using devices which can do the same things. Although students may already be familiar with each other's mobile devices, be aware that they may be concerned about comparing them in class and watch out for teasing. If a student doesn't have their own device, make them the reporter, whose job is to listen and report back on interesting facts they hear.

Try this ☞ **What can my device do?**

On the board, write a list of things a mobile device can typically allow you to do, such as send messages, take photos, search the internet, record audio, play games, etc. Ask students to talk in small groups about what their devices can and can't do and which features they use most. Link what students tell you about how they use their devices to what you will be doing in class. For example, explain that they can take photos outside the classroom as well as inside for use in language activities, to bring more personalization to their learning. Having discussed how mobile devices can improve their learning experience, it is important to stress that students will only be allowed to use them in accordance with school policy (see Chapter 2).

✓ **Getting it right** | **Change language settings**

Ask students to change the display language on their mobile device to English – they should be able to do this in 'settings'. This is one way of making sure that their mobile use in class is focused on learning the target language.

Why this works ▶ **Talking about functions**

Finding out what your students know and don't know about operating a device will help in planning activities, and will give a better idea of how much input will be required to get all students up to speed. It's also an excellent icebreaker for new classes, as students will get to know each other through group discussion.

Mobile learning and 21st century skills

Mobile technologies can be used to enhance 21st century skills in the classroom. These skills, often known as the four Cs (creativity, critical thinking, communication, collaboration), can all be developed in student-centred, dynamic, and motivating ways.

Creativity and critical thinking

There are many ways in which mobile learning can develop creativity. It's particularly suited to project work, since students can work anywhere and collaborate online outside the classroom, as well as face-to-face in class. They can research information on the internet or call on expert advice via Twitter or other forums. Students can work together to create magazines, e-books, and videos in 2D or even 3D, then use their mobile devices to present their ideas online or in person.

Learning to deal with a wealth of information, and deciding what is correct and what isn't helps students to develop their critical thinking skills. When they conduct online research, they build these skills – for example, through choosing effective search terms, evaluating materials, and deciding how to adapt and use the information they find.

Communication and collaboration

Mobile learning also helps students to focus on communication and collaboration. For example, students can connect through messaging outside the classroom. They can chat, ask questions, discuss ideas, and share work via the class website, all through their mobile devices. Messaging apps can be used for quickly sharing media, such as photos, during a lesson (assuming everyone is connected to the same network). WhatsApp is a popular **cross-platform** mobile messaging app that allows people to send messages without having to pay for an SMS (short message service or text message). Other such apps include Kik, Facebook Messenger, and Viber.

Digital literacy

Digital literacy can be defined as the knowledge of digital tools combined with the ability to evaluate information and socially engage with it. The skills needed on both an individual and social level to deal with these digital tools are known as digital literacies, which can be broken down into various categories. For example, information literacy involves knowing where and how to find, use, and evaluate information, while media literacy refers to the ability to deal with different text types and genres. Remix literacy is about reusing audio, images, video, etc. to create something new.

In order to effectively carry out online research, students need to be digitally literate. They need to be able to evaluate the information they find to determine how useful it is. This involves understanding what the context of the source of information is; for example, is it an academic paper,

THINKING ABOUT GOING MOBILE

a newspaper article, an advert, or a text message? Students need to be able to interpret the information and use it to inform the work they are doing, without simply copying and pasting the information directly from the source. It is also important to be aware that copying and pasting can infringe copyright laws in some circumstances.

Try this  **Fact-finding mission**

Before the lesson, write 'fact-finding' questions on the board. Examples are given below for questions about the UK, but the activity can be adapted to any topic that appeals to your students or which is relevant to your learning focus.

1. What is the UK flag called?
2. What are the national flowers of England, Scotland, and Wales?
3. What is the second most spoken language in the UK?
4. What is the 26th December called in the UK?
5. What are the national sports of England, Scotland, and Wales?
6. Which foods are considered the UK's national dishes?

Answers:

1. The Union Jack or Union Flag
2. England: rose; Scotland: thistle; Wales: daffodil
3. Polish
4. Boxing Day
5. England: cricket or football; Scotland and Wales: rugby or football
6. Possible answers: fish and chips, Sunday roast, full English breakfast, chicken tikka masala

Ask students to open a **browser** on their mobile device. Give them a time limit to find the answers and write them down or type them in a note-taking app, also noting where they found the answer. Then get students to compare answers in pairs or small groups before checking as a class. Their searches may return different answers, but the important thing is that they can justify them. Students can then work in groups to make their own quiz for the class and share it using a group messaging app.

 **Group messaging**

Find out which messenger apps are popular in your country. You could do this by asking students which they use and discussing the advantages and disadvantages of each app. Having decided which one to use, you can set up different groups and use group messaging with each class you teach. It's a quick and easy way to share information, post questions, and set homework.

Getting it right **Navigating the internet**

To get the most from an internet search, try the following:
- Use double quotation marks (" ") around specific phrases you want to search for so that only pages with those exact words appear.
- Use an asterisk as a 'wildcard' symbol to search for words that start with the same letters; for example, *instruct** will find *instruct, instructs, instructor*, etc.

15

Getting the classroom ready

For many of the activities in this book, you will only need the mobile device itself, so you should ideally be able to walk into your classroom, ask the students to take out their mobile devices, and begin teaching. However, a well-equipped classroom can really enhance mobile learning. Exactly what you need depends on how your school approaches the use of mobile devices, but a strong wi-fi network is usually important. Schools that provide class or student sets of devices need to ensure that they can keep them charged and their **software** up to date; this is typically the responsibility of an IT staff member. All devices should have the same software installed on them so that if you need to work with a particular app, for example, you can be certain it will be there. As we shall see in later chapters, different devices have similar features such as cameras and browsers, but certain apps are specifically designed for use on one particular operating system and won't work on others.

Most mobile devices use one of three main operating systems – iOS, Android, or Windows. The iOS operating system was developed by Apple for use on its iPhones and iPads. Apple develops both software and **hardware**, while Android runs on several types of mobile device, including those created by Amazon, Google, and Samsung. Some mobile devices, such as Microsoft Surface, run a version of Windows.

Bring your own device (BYOD)

Some schools follow a 'bring your own device' policy. BYOD is a popular and cost-effective way of introducing mobile learning in a school where students are allowed to use their own device in class. For BYOD to be successful, all students need to have access to a device. To make this possible, some schools offer a school lease or purchase scheme.

The advantage of BYOD is that students will be comfortable using their devices. However, there is no guarantee that they will already have or want to download particular apps you wish to use, especially if there is a cost attached. Moreover, as mentioned above, different devices have different capabilities, and not all apps will necessarily work on the different operating systems.

Compatibility

In the BYOD classroom, the most obvious question to raise is whether a particular app works on all types of device. If not, then how will you use it? This might not rule out use altogether, as it may not be necessary for all students to have the app. As we shall see later, when mobile devices are used in group work, it is often the case that only one device is needed per group.

Using the teacher's device

Teachers may use their own device as the only one in the classroom. Although not essential, connecting it to a projector means that students

THINKING ABOUT GOING MOBILE

can easily see what's on your screen. Most (but not all) mobile devices will connect to a projector if you have the correct **adaptor**. You can usually find out which one you need by visiting the manufacturer's website. Depending on the age of both the device and the projector, you will need either a **VGA** adaptor or an **HDMI** adaptor.

Once you have connected an adaptor cable to your device and projector, the projector should automatically pick up and display an enlarged version of the device screen.

If the projector in your classroom is already linked to a computer or an interactive whiteboard, it can be awkward to remove the cable from the computer each time you want to project the screen of your mobile device. One solution is to install a program on the computer that will display your mobile device screen. These programs work by making use of a wi-fi network to connect a mobile device and a computer. Popular programs include Droid@Screen for Android and X-Mirage for Apple (bear in mind that there may be a small cost). Once the program is installed and running on the computer, it will 'mirror' (i.e. display) your device screen on the computer. And if the computer is already connected to a data projector, your mobile screen will then be projected onto the projector screen or wall. By mirroring, you can continue to use the device while 'broadcasting' what you do on the larger screen. Mirroring is an excellent way to display a video from your device on a bigger screen, for example to show how an app or program works, or to create a platform for reviewing students' work.

If all the devices being used in the classroom are Apple, using an Apple TV box will allow anyone connected to the box via wi-fi to send content from their device to a big screen using AirPlay. You can do the same with Android devices using the Amazon Fire TV box. If your classroom has a TV, an alternative to the box is a **dongle** such as Google Chromecast. This fits into the HDMI port on a TV and allows for the mirroring of video from any device and selected content from Android devices.

 *Getting it right*

Protecting your data

If you use a password to lock your device, remember to enter it *before* you display your screen; otherwise, everyone will be able to see it. Also make sure to close any apps you don't want students to see – so you don't accidentally share your social media profiles, for example.

Wi-fi

While wi-fi is needed for many things, such as connecting devices, sharing photos and documents, and accessing the internet, it isn't always necessary. Most apps, for example, don't need wi-fi to run. However, if you want the students to be able to conduct research or to access and play a video online, then you will need wi-fi or an alternative way to connect to the internet. Devices with a SIM card can connect to mobile phone networks, enabling internet access without the need for wi-fi. Almost all phones come with a SIM card and a **data package**. But while some countries provide generous data amounts, others do not, and students may not be happy about using their own data packages for class use.

 **Getting it right**

> **Secure wi-fi access**
>
> If you can access your school's wi-fi network, talk to your IT department about blocking sites you don't want students to access. It is also possible to create a separate network so students can connect to the internet more securely and to protect the main network from potential security risks such as viruses or hacking.

Other equipment

It's a good idea to have a set of speakers to play audio from your device. In most classroom settings, the internal speakers of the device will not produce enough volume for everyone to hear clearly.

 **Getting it right**

> **Headphones**
>
> For some tasks, you might want students to work independently with headphones. This allows students to pause, rewind, and replay audio as they wish, rather than being limited to how often the teacher decides to play it. Students can get more from listening texts this way, which can in turn boost their confidence.

You don't need a lot of equipment to get started with mobile devices. As we explore different activities, you will see which equipment will be most useful to you.

Storing and sharing work

Internet access is essential for sharing and storing work. When students complete a piece of work on paper, you collect it in; and when you make a worksheet on paper, you hand it out. With mobile devices, you need a way of collecting in and handing out work digitally. A relatively easy way to store or distribute work is using a 'cloud' site. Cloud sites work by giving online storage space, which you access through a browser or app. They also make it easy to share files and documents. Popular cloud sites such as Dropbox, iCloud, and OneDrive offer a limited amount of free storage space, which will be enough to get you started. On the site, you will need to create a folder that each class can access.

There is also a range of storage and sharing apps aimed at helping teachers create paperless classrooms. Examples include Showbie and Schoology, which allow teachers to create spaces for each of their classes.

THINKING ABOUT GOING MOBILE

Why this works ▶ **Using mobile devices**
Mobile devices can be used as a springboard for language practice and real-life communication. They can help students to evaluate their own learning and analyse the quality of their language production, as well as capture and understand language in the world beyond the classroom. Mobile devices also open the door to all kinds of media creation which can then be easily shared, empowering students to demonstrate their language abilities and take control of their own learning.

2 Getting started

Preparing the way

Having decided to incorporate mobile devices into your teaching, it is time to consider how you are going to use them in the classroom. If the school is implementing a mobile device policy, the students will already be aware of this because the school should have informed them and their parents/carers. However, as discussed in Chapter 1, you will still need to clarify with your students how and why mobile devices can help them with their learning.

When to use mobile devices

It has been argued that students who use their mobile devices in class tend to write down less information, remember less, and perform worse on a multiple-choice test than students who don't use them. Make sure you adopt a principled approach to their use. When planning each lesson, consider these questions:
- What is the learning aim for students?
- How will mobile devices help students to achieve this aim?
- What will be my role when they are using the devices?
- How will I control their use?

Your answers should help you decide whether or not the use of mobile devices in an activity is justified.

Acceptable use policies

Bring your own device (BYOD)

The school needs a clear policy if it is implementing a BYOD scheme. Teachers will need to be trained in dealing with the implications of students using their own mobile devices in class. While some teachers may have reservations about BYOD, once one teacher allows mobile device use in class, they create a precedent for others. Stakeholders, including students' parents/carers, need to be informed and consulted before the planned start date. It is important to educate them in matters such as ensuring that students' devices are clearly identifiable and are appropriately insured in the event of loss or damage.

GETTING STARTED 2

Creating an acceptable use policy

Whether students are using their own or the school's devices, it is important to create an 'acceptable use policy' with them. This is an official document which provides guidelines on what students can and can't do with mobile devices in class and with the school's wi-fi. It should cover which sites students can access and what they can upload to or download from in class, as well as smaller details such as when they should have their devices on silent mode. Students should also be clear about what will happen if they don't follow the agreed policy. Consider carefully which areas you need to cover – an internet search on what other schools provide might be helpful. Typically, you will want to address the following areas.

Assigning responsibility: With a school-owned device, what happens if it is broken or lost? For BYOD, make sure to clarify that the school isn't responsible for students' own devices.

When to use devices: This should clarify when students can and cannot use their devices, and what they can and cannot be used for. For example, you should include guidelines on when it is acceptable to record audio or video, or take photos of fellow students. This needs to cover how the end result will be shared and getting permission from students (or their parents/carers) to be recorded or filmed. When connected to the school wi-fi, you need to decide whether to restrict access to certain sites or prohibit students from uploading images and videos. Think carefully about what the consequences of breaking the rules will be. Will you confiscate the device? If so, when will you return it? What will happen to students who repeatedly break the rules?

Try this ☞ **Set the rules together**

Create an 'acceptable use' policy for the classroom with your students. This will also provide an opportunity for them to think about the learning process. Explain that you want to work on a class contract to provide rules for acceptable mobile device use in class. Give them a few minutes to brainstorm their own rules, then write them on the board, adding any you wish to include. Discuss and agree on a final list. Finally, students should write or type up the rules to make a class poster. Display this for the duration of the year and refer to it when necessary.

✓ **Getting it right** | **Follow through**
Some students may 'test' the rules by breaking them. Make sure you follow through with the agreed consequences and remind them that you set the rules together. Should a rule prove too difficult to follow, you can renegotiate with the class and amend it appropriately.

Why this works  | **Getting students on board**
By creating a class contract together, you are involving students in the decision-making process. This should ensure that they understand and are happy to accept the final policy, which in turn should make them more likely to abide by it.

Dealing with distraction

You need to consider how you will deal with the distractions that mobile device use can cause – for example, what to do about students using them to answer personal texts or access **social networks**. You might also want devices to operate on silent mode to avoid the interruptions of text alerts and ring tones.

Try this ☞ **Traffic lights**

Search the **app store** on your mobile device for traffic light apps. These are simple but effective tools to help with classroom management, by making it clear when students are allowed to use their mobile devices; a green light means they can, and a red light means they can't. Though you could simply show students your device screen, traffic light apps are most effective when they are projected or mirrored onto a bigger screen so that students can see the light at a glance.

Try this ☞ **Activity timer**

The traffic light app can also be used as an activity timer. For example, ask students to talk for five minutes about photos they have on their devices. Set the traffic light to green and the timer for five minutes before the light changes to red. A green light means the task is in progress, and a red light means it's time to stop. You can even set the timer to move from green to amber to red, with amber signalling, for example, that the speaker should change.

Why this works 
> **Maintaining the flow**
> Using the traffic lights system means that you needn't interrupt the flow of an activity with verbal instructions. It also allows you to concentrate on monitoring students doing the activity, rather than monitoring device use.

✓ **Getting it right**
> **Put away your devices**
> When mobile devices aren't required, tell students to put them away. If the 'put away and take out' strategy is a distraction in itself, ask them to put the devices on their desks with the screen facing down. This is the same in principle as closing a book.

✓ **Getting it right**
> **Airplane mode**
> Another way to limit distraction is using **airplane mode**, which prevents a device from connecting to a phone or wi-fi network. In this mode, students won't be able to send texts or connect to the internet.

Staying safe

If we are encouraging mobile device use in class, we have a duty to ensure our students' safety. We need to teach them how to navigate the internet safely and make them aware of the consequences of what they do online.

We may assume that because students use mobile devices and go online outside the classroom, they know how to do this safely. But they may not be aware that what they do is often tracked, recorded, and monitored.

Everything we do online – every click of a button and every photo we tag – leaves a data trail, sometimes known as a **digital footprint**. This footprint is an online representation of ourselves, and it is important to understand how to manage it responsibly and effectively.

Make sure students know how to keep their personal details safe and understand the possible consequences of sharing photos. Talk to them about how to deal with anyone (fellow student or stranger) who sends them unwanted or offensive messages. And don't forget to include basic information such as how to lock a device and raise awareness of which apps can track you.

Try this  **Safety can-do quiz**

A simple way to find out what students know is by creating a 'can-do' quiz with questions such as the following:

How do you ...
- set a passcode?
- find out what apps are tracking you?
- turn on auto-lock?
- ensure that you are logged out of social networking sites such as Facebook?
- close apps?

Ask students to see how many things they can and can't do before going through the list in pairs, teaching each other anything they couldn't do. If neither student can do something, ask them to find someone in the class who can.

Cyberbullying

Unfortunately, the proliferation of mobile devices has led to an increase in cyberbullying. This refers to the use of text messages, emails, social networking sites, online forums, chat rooms, etc. to insult, threaten, or humiliate another person. An example of this might be sharing and uploading photos without a person's consent, or writing offensive comments on a person's web page or social media profile.

✓ *Getting it right* **Protocols for bullying**

Ensure that your acceptable use policy covers cyberbullying and discuss it with the students. There are many useful resources on the internet, including downloadable information sheets from the National Crime Prevention Council (NCPC) website.

Using apps

With over two million mobile apps available, it is perhaps unsurprising that, although they open up a world of opportunities, teachers may feel overwhelmed and find it difficult to know where to begin. Common questions are:
- How do I find apps?
- What are good apps for language learning?
- How do I know they are the right level?
- Which learning apps do students really like?

Before we set about answering these questions, we need to remember that mobile learning isn't necessarily about using apps we have downloaded from the app store. There are plenty of things we can ask students to do with their mobile devices using the most basic features and apps that they are already likely to be familiar with (see Chapter 3).

The first thing you need to be clear about is that you are choosing an app that will help students learn more effectively than if you were using traditional classroom tools. Look carefully at what an app does and what it requires you to do. For example, if it only provides the same type of language practice as a coursebook or workbook, then recommend it to students who want extra practice at home.

The SAMR model

One way to help you decide if an app or a piece of technology is useful for your students is the **SAMR** model, devised by Ruben Puentedura. (See *Useful apps and websites* for a link to Puentedura's blog on applying the SAMR model.)

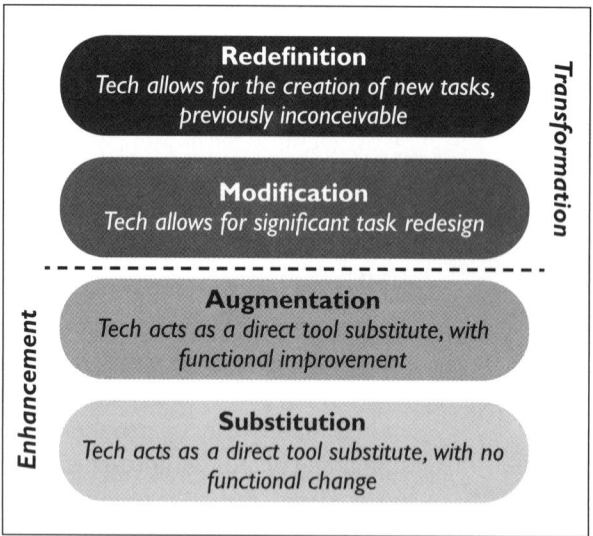

FIGURE 2.1   *The SAMR model*

Many gap-fill apps fit into the **S**ubstitution category. When students do a gap-fill activity on their mobile device rather than in a book, the app simply substitutes the teacher input and practice of the language for a more personalized approach. **A**ugmentation applies when the change adds something else; for example, using a vocabulary app to record and listen to yourself saying new vocabulary, as well as recording its written form.

No radical changes are achieved in the first two categories, but technology can have a dramatic effect on how we teach and learn. **M**odification and **R**edefinition apply when technology allows us to do things that would not be possible otherwise.

 **Getting it right** | **Less is more**
Beware of using too many different apps in class, as you may lose sight of what you are trying to teach. Make sure you know what you want to achieve with each app that you use, and how it will contribute to more effective learning.

Choosing an app

Since there are millions of apps and not all are available for all devices, this book avoids naming specific apps where possible, concentrating instead on types of activity. However, some apps will be recommended as a starting point or because of their widespread use in education.

✓ **Getting it right** | **How easy is it to use?**
You don't want the way an app works to get in the way of the learning process, so avoid ones that are complicated to use. Some apps take a long time to set up, often requiring the creation of an account, user name verification, and so on. If the app is going to take the students more than a couple of minutes to set up and start using, then you should question its value for use in class. Likewise, if the app is complicated to use, this will be off-putting and almost certainly take the focus off language practice and production.

How motivating is it?

In language learning, task motivation is determined by the interest in doing an activity and the desire it stimulates to produce language, and it is vitally important for any tool we use in the language classroom. This includes app use. Broadly speaking, we can divide apps for the language classroom into two categories: those which offer automated language practice and those which enable users to create things. The former tend to be apps for practising grammar or vocabulary, which give an automated response as to whether you have done something correctly or not. Creative apps allow students to make things using the language, such as an e-book, poster, or video. Both have their place in language learning, but overuse of automated apps in the classroom may lead to demotivation among students. As a rule of thumb, the more an app asks students to create, the more likely it is to be engaging and therefore lead to increased task motivation.

✓ **Getting it right** | **Free apps**
Make sure you know what you're getting with free apps. Some are **freemium**, which means they allow you to download a basic version for free, then make you pay to unlock more advanced (and more useful) features. Free apps often contain advertising, so check what kinds of adverts are being shown first and decide whether they are appropriate for your class. Finally, if the app asks for an email address, be aware that this may result in your students receiving unwanted email spam.

Try this  **An app evaluation form**
App evaluation forms are a useful way to record what you think about a particular app, which you can share with other members of staff. It is easy to draw up your own form so the questions are tailored to your needs, but you can use Figure 2.2 as a starting point.

App name: _____

Suitable operating systems: iOS / Android / Windows

Suitable devices: Phone / Tablet / Both

Purpose of app: _____

Quick questions

Is the app engaging?	Yes / No
Can you get started immediately or do you have to create an account?	Yes / No
Is it user-friendly?	Yes / No
Is it free?	Yes / No
Does it contain advertising?	Yes / No
Does the app give the student feedback?	Yes / No
Is it for individual or collaborative work?	Yes / No
Is it for use in or out of class?	In / Out / Both
Do students produce anything?	Yes / No

If so, what? _____

How will it be shared? _____

What skills does it focus on? _____

How will the app benefit a lesson or benefit language production?

FIGURE 2.2   *App evaluation form*

Photocopiable © Oxford University Press

Why this works ⇒ **Smart use**

Smartphones and other mobile devices can be distracting, but don't let this deter you from using them in class. When backed up by a carefully considered acceptable use policy, mobile devices encourage better engagement and learning. A clear policy on when students can use them in class separates device time from other tasks and activities, ensuring that the focus always remains on language learning. Mobile devices also offer flexibility and efficiency. For example, just as you might ask students to use a dictionary to clarify unknown words, with mobile devices you can ask them to do quick research online. Ultimately, using mobile devices is faster than going through the process of accessing school computers, even if these are readily available, freeing up more time for learning.

Part 2 Taking the first steps

3 Take out your devices

Using mobile devices with students does not have to be complicated. As noted in Chapter 2, there is no need to equate mobile devices with the millions of apps that can be downloaded from the app store. While many of these apps are useful, as we shall see in later chapters, it's important not to overlook the most basic apps and features that students may already be using on their devices. In this chapter, we will explore some activities that make use of these.

Text messaging

Let's begin with a quick quiz! Feel free to use your mobile device to find the answers.
1 What did the first text message ever sent say?
2 How many characters can you use in an SMS text message in English?
3 When is the best time to send a text message to ensure that it is read by the receiver?
4 Does texting improve your language?

It should not have taken you too long to find the answers with a quick internet search.

Answers:
1 The first text message said 'Merry Christmas'. It was sent in 1992.
2 SMS text messages are limited to 160 characters. Messaging apps on smart devices allow for much longer messages.
3 Studies show that the peak hours for sending and reading text messages are from 10.30–11.30 p.m.
4 There has been much debate as to whether texting is good or bad for language development. In order to save time and use fewer characters, many people use 'textspeak'. Some argue that this has led to a decline in literacy, with teenagers failing to learn how to write properly. Others claim that the changes introduced by textspeak are destroying languages. On the other hand, some people suggest that primary school students who text are actually better spellers than those who don't, and that knowing the conventions of text messaging (textisms) makes you more aware of grammar and genre.

Your students are likely to text in their own language, and will probably be keen to text in English, too. So textspeak is something we can usefully teach them.

Try this ☞ **Translating textspeak**
Before class, prepare a list of textspeak you want to teach (do an internet search on 'text language dictionaries' to find relevant resources). In class, make sure students understand the difference between abbreviations and acronyms,

TAKE OUT YOUR DEVICES

and check whether they know what an emoticon is. Now give students some examples of textspeak and ask them to say (or guess) what they mean. Then put students into teams and give each team a mobile device with access to a **chat group**. Post an example of textspeak and tell students that the first team to type the correct meaning in the chat group will win a point. Repeat with other items. The team with the most points wins. To follow up, ask students to text further examples for others to guess.

Here are some examples:

1   2moro   6   BFF
2   GR8   7   NP
3   IMO   8   BRB
4   B4N   9   SOZ
5   LOL   10 L8R

Answers: 1 tomorrow   2 great   3 in my opinion   4 bye for now
5 laugh out loud   6 best friend forever   7 no problem   8 be right back
9 sorry   10 later

 **Getting it right**

Setting up a chat group

Text messaging isn't always free. Be aware that in a BYOD class, students might be unwilling to send texts they have to pay for. If your school has wi-fi, you can use online messaging services such as Apple's iMessage to send free messages. You can also use a chat group. Setting up a chat group on a messaging app is relatively easy. With Apple's iMessage, for example, you simply add people to the message to create a group for future use. If you are using a chat group app, most follow a similar procedure. Open the app, start a chat, and you should see an option to create a group. You can then add students to the group.

Nowadays, people may spend more time typing on a device than writing with a pen or pencil. While the skill of handwriting remains important, text messaging is another way of writing that can be used to motivate students and give new life to some traditional classroom activities, from simple dictations to story writing. The activities below demonstrate how these traditional favourites can be played within a chat group. Chat groups also offer potential to extend the game beyond the classroom.

Why this works

Keep on learning

Having a chat group means activities started in a lesson can be continued out of class, which makes it a good way to keep students engaged and motivated to learn in their own time. Once the chat group is established, you can use it for many different activities.

Try this   **Text message dictation**

Find a short text from your coursebook – for example, part of a reading text or an audioscript. Ask students to open the text messaging function or app on their device and start a new message. Tell them you are going to dictate a short text, which they should type (using textspeak if they wish). Ask them to compare their completed texts with each other. Then ask them to compare their texts with the original and discuss any differences, including any textspeak they have used.

Try this 👉 **Guess my word**

Open the chat group and send a message that describes a word recently covered in class. Invite students to guess what it is. For example: 'It's a thing you carry around with you and use to make and receive calls. Can anyone guess what it is?' Ask students to post their answers in the chat group. The first student to guess correctly posts a description of another word for their classmates to guess, and so on. The activity could go on for several days!

Try this 👉 **Adapting word games**

Use a chat group to play word chain games, where students take turns to add a new word; for example, 'I went to the market and I bought ...'. This adaptation changes the focus of the original game, which is to memorize a list of words, and is useful for revising a previously taught lexical set. You can also use chat groups to revise vocabulary through word association games, where students have to think of a word that relates to the previous word. For example, if the first word is 'teacher', the next person might add 'student', the next 'classroom', and so on. If a student types a word that doesn't seem to obviously fit, you can ask them to provide an explanation in brackets. Add other rules and challenges to keep students engaged and motivated, such as keeping a record of the longest chains or allowing students to only add another word after all students in the class have given one.

Try this 👉 **Collaborative stories**

Give students an opening phrase to begin their story (for example, 'Once upon a time'). Tell them they are going to continue the story, using only five words at a time. Ask them to work in small groups with one mobile device per group. The first student adds their words, then passes the device to the left so the next student can add to the story. The story should end when the device has returned to the first person in the group. Students then read their stories aloud to the class and vote on which story they like best. Ask students to send you the final texts so you can use them for further language work, such as error correction.

Why this works ⇒ | **Crafting a message**
Replacing traditional activities with ones using mobile devices can engage students who see such activities as old-fashioned and dull. Being able to understand and deliver information clearly in small chunks is part of everyday life – from email marketing to newsfeeds on social networking sites or information shared on Twitter. Collaborative story writing requires students to decide what to include and what to leave out so that the text is as clear, coherent, and concise as possible. Typing rather than writing on paper also allows you to edit the text easily, deleting and rewriting as often as necessary.

Micro stories, also known as 'txtlit' and 'twitterature', are complete stories told using the SMS text limit of 160 characters. Ask students to write micro stories inside and outside the classroom for some great creative language practice; you could even encourage them to enter micro story competitions.

Try this 👉 **Micro stories**

Ask students to plan and type a micro story in small groups, using one mobile device per group. You can adapt the micro story to match the students' age and language level, and focus on a particular language point. For example, review past tenses by getting students to write a story in the past simple. Alternatively, give them a theme (for example, 'Summer') or have them include a particular vocabulary item. Once students have finished typing their stories, ask each group to read their story aloud to the class. The Txtlit website has lots of examples you can use to introduce the idea. Figure 3.1 shows a couple of classroom examples.

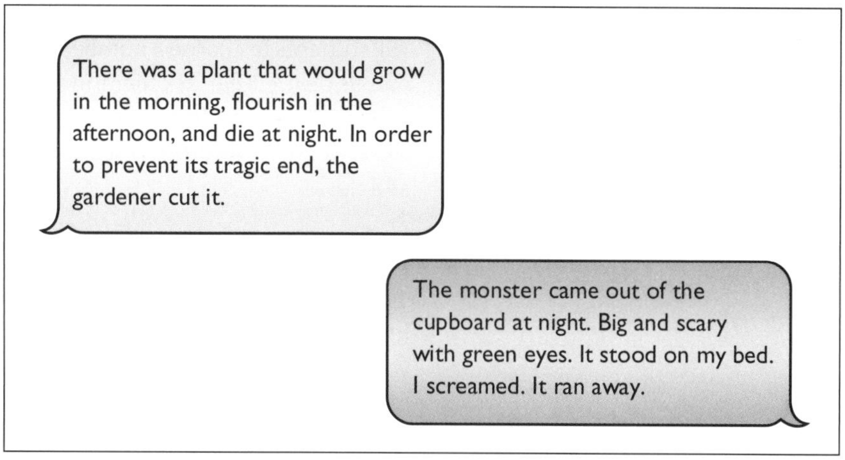

> There was a plant that would grow in the morning, flourish in the afternoon, and die at night. In order to prevent its tragic end, the gardener cut it.

> The monster came out of the cupboard at night. Big and scary with green eyes. It stood on my bed. I screamed. It ran away.

FIGURE 3.1 *Micro stories*

Emoji

Do you know your 😛 from your 👻 ?

If not, you can look them up in the online dictionary Emojipedia. These small digital icons, known as **emoji**, originated from Japan and differ from **emoticons** in that they are images rather than typographical characters. For example, a wink as an emoji is 😉 and as an emoticon ;-).

Emoji have been used in electronic messages and on web pages since the late 1990s, but their popularity has grown with the rise in use of social networks and mobile devices. There are over 1,600 emoji characters representing all manner of things, from facial expressions to everyday objects and weather symbols; the average mobile device allows users to access around 800. New emoji are reviewed and added by an approved committee each year. If you want to see what will be added, search online for 'new emoji' and follow the links.

The rapid growth of emoji use is partly due to the fact that they can save time keying in characters when sending a message. Another reason is that a picture can express more than a cluster of words – especially as pictures can transcend cultural borders, unlike text. Emoji also help to personalize a message. Since electronic messages tend to look the same, they can seem impersonal, so adding emoji allows the sender to give their message a personal feel.

If you have never used emoji, open a messaging app on your mobile device and look at the on-screen keyboard. You should be able to access the emoji keyboard via one of the keys near the space bar. If not, search the internet for '[your device type] and emoji' to find instructions.

As with text messaging, emoji can provide a motivating stimulus for language practice among students. For example, you can use emoji as the basis for a speaking activity, or to revise vocabulary.

Try this **What does it mean?**

Ask students to choose a number of emoji from a messaging app on their mobile device. Then ask them, in pairs, to decide what each emoji means, giving reasons. For example, for the 'ghost' emoji on page 33, they may say 'ghost', 'Halloween', or 'surprise'. Discuss the various meanings students came up with as a class.

Try this **Guess the emoji**

Open a messaging app on your mobile device, start a new message with the heading 'Guess the emoji', and use emoji to represent the word or phrase that you want the students to guess. Some examples are shown in Figure 3.2, and you can find more ideas on emoji translation websites.

Send students the message or, if you can, project or mirror your screen. Ask them to guess the meaning of the emoji and type their answers back to you. You can play this game in a number of different ways; for example, you could award points for correct answers; or you could allow the first student with a correct answer to send the next emoji. As a follow up, ask students to think of their own emoji representations for words and phrases covered in lessons. They can send them to other students via text messaging or the class chat group.

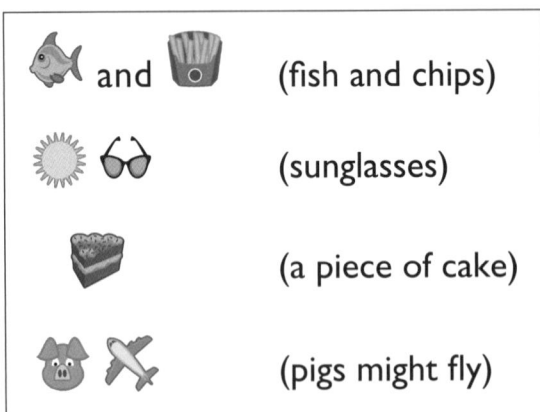

FIGURE 3.2 *Emoji words and phrases*

Why this works ▶ | **Crossing cultural borders**
Emoji are a global form of communication because they cross cultural borders, although full understanding will depend on the overall context of the message. You can see a real-time snapshot of emoji in use and which are most popular in different countries by visiting the Emoji tracker website.

Another way to use emoji is in a rebus activity, where words are represented by images. Can you guess the nursery rhyme in Figure 3.3?

FIGURE 3.3 *Emoji rebus*

Answer:
Twinkle twinkle little star
How I wonder what you are
Up above the world so high
Like a diamond in the sky

Try this ☞ | **Complete a rebus**
Create or find a rebus before the lesson (for ideas, search online for 'rebus nursery rhymes'). If your students are too old for nursery rhymes, use song lyrics. Show students an example and explain that they are going to create their own rebus. Choose a nursery rhyme or song together and discuss which words (for example, nouns) you might replace with emoji. Using a projector or an interactive whiteboard, write a few lines, replacing some words with emoji. Put the students into groups, with one device per group, and tell them to do the same for the rest of the rhyme or song. The groups then compare their rebuses. Did they use the same emoji? Did some use more emoji than others?

Try this ☞ | **Write your own rebus story**
Ask students to create their own rebus stories in groups. Do this in one lesson, or over a series of lessons so that students can develop their stories outside class. Tell them to collaborate in a chat group to plan what they will show and what text to include. Ask students to share their finished rebus stories for their

classmates to decode. They can send their stories as a text message or capture it as a screenshot and share it as an image, via text messaging or in a class chat group. Groups decode each other's stories and send them back to the creators to check their answer.

 **Getting it right** | **Screenshots**
How to take a screenshot varies from one mobile device to another. Search the internet for '[your device type] and screenshot' to find instructions.

Games

Most students enjoy playing games on their mobile devices, and you can tap into this enthusiasm by creating some useful language-related games which practise, for example, giving instructions or advice, making recommendations, sequencing events, etc.

Try this | **Explain my game**
In a BYOD class, ask students to choose a game they are currently playing on their device or have played recently. Ask them to work in groups and explain their games to each other, saying if they would recommend them. Encourage students to ask each other questions about how the games work to make sure they all understand. You could ask students to make an audio recording or a video of their interviews using their mobile devices (see Chapters 6 and 8) so they can discuss each other's contributions.

Try this | **Game reviews**
Ask students to write mobile game reviews. They can build up a 'library' of reviews and/or provide a weekly recommendation for other students. They can use a word processor on their mobile devices to write reviews to share via an online noticeboard (see Chapter 5) – in keeping with the fact that game reviews and information can be found online. They can also use their mobile devices to compose their reviews as posts on the class website.

Audio recording

Before mobile devices existed, recording students or having them record themselves was often time-consuming and expensive. Mobile devices capture reasonably high-quality audio, which can be a useful classroom resource. If the mobile device you are using doesn't have an inbuilt audio recording function, search for free apps in the app store on your device by typing in 'audio recorder' or 'video recorder'. We will look at more complex uses later in the book (see Chapters 6 and 8), but let us first consider perhaps the most straightforward and productive way to use an audio recorder, which is to record students doing a speaking task.

Try this **Recording for self-assessment**

Ask students to record a class speaking activity on their mobile device. Then ask them to listen to their recordings and evaluate their own performance to decide how they could improve it. Monitor the activity so you have an idea of how well students performed. Help them make their language more natural and give them any new vocabulary and language structures they need. Then ask them to repeat the speaking task and record it again. Finally, students should compare the two recordings to see if they have improved.

Getting it right **Helping students to self-assess**

The first time you ask students to do self- or peer assessment, you may need to guide them on how to evaluate themselves and each other. Give them questions about how well they think they performed. For example:
1 Is it easy to hear and understand all your words?
2 Did you notice any grammar mistakes?
3 Did you notice any problems with specific sounds?
4 How did you sound? Interesting? Bored? Enthusiastic?
5 Did you speak naturally or did you pause a lot?
6 Were your ideas organized and easy for others to follow?
7 Did you complete the task?

You don't have to use all the questions each time; use them as a framework and choose one or two to focus on. Though some students might not feel confident about evaluating themselves at first, they will find it easier each time you do this activity with them. You can also reassure them that you are always there to help.

Why this works **Make the most of speaking**

Our feedback for class speaking activities is often based on the performance of a select number of students, due to time constraints. This means the feedback is likely to be rather general. Allowing students to record themselves gives them more focus as individuals, increasing their motivation. It also gives students more control over their learning because, by repeating the task, they will hear improvements in their language use – which is motivating, too.

Getting it right **Be sensitive to shy students**

Not all students will enjoy being recorded. Some may have concerns about privacy, and others are simply shy. Reassure them that all recordings will be deleted before the lesson ends. (You would need to do this anyway unless you had written permission from the students to keep their work.) If these students are still reluctant to speak, make them the 'teacher'. In other words, allow them to do the recording, and in the evaluating stages, ask them to keep track of which language points need further attention.

Audio recording can be used in all kinds of speaking tasks. Ask students to record pronunciation activities from the coursebook so they can judge for themselves how well they produce sounds and whether their word stress is correct. They can also record themselves reading dialogues to evaluate their intonation.

Why this works ▶

> **Engaging substitution**
>
> Most of the activities in this chapter belong in the substitution and augmentation categories of the SAMR model (see Chapter 2). Using mobile devices in this way may not be innovative, but it is certainly effective. By drawing on activity types that students are comfortable with, we can reduce the stress of introducing mobile learning into the classroom.

4 A photo tells a thousand words

The previous chapter looked at some of the most basic features of mobile devices and how they might be used in class. This chapter looks at perhaps the most popular feature – the camera. While photos have long been an integral aid in language teaching, teachers were limited to using physical photos until fairly recently. Nowadays, most mobile devices can take photos, and students are likely to enter the classroom with their device full of pictures, which can be used for both language production and skills work. By asking students to take photos inside and outside class to use in lessons, you allow them to bring their own lives into the classroom, personalizing materials and making tasks more intrinsically motivating.

Selfies

Mobile devices may have contributed to the decline of the traditional camera, but they are also responsible for the rise of new phenomena such as the **selfie**.

Try this **A selfie icebreaker**

Use this activity with a new class as an icebreaker or a 'getting to know you' activity. Write 'selfie' on the board and ask students what it means and what they think about selfies. Then ask students to take selfies using their devices. Let them decide how to take their photos – whether to include other students, for example. Then ask students to walk round the class and show their selfies to each other. Encourage them to comment on each other's selfies and ask questions (why they posed the way they did, etc.). Follow up by discussing with the class whether selfies are a positive or negative thing. Ask students to share their photos with you by email or in a chat group. You can either print off the photos for display on the classroom wall as a selfie gallery or, if you have a class website or blog, display them there.

Try this **Who am I?**

Ask students to take three or four selfies for homework. Each photo should reflect something about their lives, hobbies, or interests (for example, doing a particular sport or activity, at home with family, out with friends, etc.). In the next class, ask students to show each other their photos in small groups and to ask questions about them. At the end of the activity, students share what they have found out with the whole class. The photos can then be added to any group site that the class is using as a starting point for further activities.

4   A PHOTO TELLS A THOUSAND WORDS

✓ Getting it right

Taking photos

If you want students to take photos of each other or to take them yourself, you will most likely need to get their permission or from their parents/carers if they are children. In most countries, data protection laws forbid the use of photos and videos taken without permission. You will need to check with your institution the exact details of the data protection laws that would apply to you and your students.

Why this works ▶

Selfies and self-esteem

Selfies are a way of presenting yourself to the world, and they have become almost second nature to many people. Some psychologists argue that they build self-confidence and self-esteem, as they usually receive positive comments from friends when shared on social networking sites. Encouraging self-confidence is key to successful language learning.

Combining photos

By using the inbuilt camera on a mobile device with downloaded apps, we can create a number of extensions and variations to tasks. One such app is a collage maker – there should be many free versions of this in your app store. A collage maker app allows you to combine several photos into one image; some also let you add text. Check that the students have a collage app (or are happy to download a free one). If they don't want to download an app, you can use your device instead and ask them to send you their photos.

Try this ☞

Odd one out

Ask students to take four photos. Three must be 'true' – that is, relevant to them in some way – and the fourth 'false'. For example, they might choose three photos that represent their hobbies and a fourth that doesn't. They then use the collage maker to combine the photos into a single image. In the next class, put students into small groups. Each student shows their collage to the other members of their group, who work together to identify the odd one out. At the end of the activity, students share what they have learned from one another's collages. Alternatively, you can display the collages on a projector one at a time and identify the odd ones out as a class activity.

A PHOTO TELLS A THOUSAND WORDS

Why this works ⟹ | **Reaching an agreement**
Asking students to take photos to share and discuss with one another not only allows for greater personalization of the topic but also leads them to work collaboratively to negotiate an outcome, an important critical thinking skill which is needed, for example, in the speaking tasks of many high-stakes exams.

Adding text

There are some simple apps you can use to augment students' photos by adding text, providing opportunities for controlled language practice.

Try this ☞ **Wanted posters**
Search for apps that create 'Wanted posters', as featured in Western films, using selfies. (If students don't want to download an app, they can send you their selfies.) Brainstorm adjectives that reflect character and write them on the board. Students take selfies and upload them to the app, adding appropriate text to their photos. The posters can be shared or uploaded to the class website.

Memes

If you have been on a social networking site recently, you are almost certain to have come across a meme. Most likely, it was a photo of a cat, some other animal, or a famous person, with a humorous remark written on it. You can use memes to practise topics and language. First, download a meme generator app – you need one that will let you add your own photos. If you want students to work on their own devices, they will need to download the app, too.

Try this ☞ **Create a meme**
After teaching or reviewing a particular language point, ask students to find or take a photo on their device that they can use to illustrate it. Add the photo to the meme generator app and get students to add text. For example, if the language point is the first conditional, then their meme could look something like Figure 4.1. Once they have added text, they should save the meme. In real life, memes are shared on social media, so encourage the students to share theirs. If you don't want them to be shared publicly, ask the students to share the memes in the class chat group.

FIGURE 4.1   *A meme using the first conditional*

Sharing photos

We have already explored ways to share work as a class, using messaging apps or by having work sent to your device to show on a projector. There are also apps for sharing photos across different devices on the same wi-fi network, such as Flick and Chirp. The user opens the app and chooses the photo they want to send. They then 'send' the photo via wi-fi and it will appear on the connected devices, as long as the intended recipients also have the app open.

Another option is to use a **closed group** function on a social network. A closed group adds a level of security for users, as only those who have been invited can access the information in the group. You can use closed groups to remind students about homework, post follow-up tasks, and share things they have missed, such as photos of notes on the whiteboard.

Instagram is a popular social networking service for sharing photos. Students can connect with their friends and upload photos using a **tag** such as *#myclass* to share them with other class members.

Getting it right — Using a closed group

If all your students are on Facebook, there is no need to set up a class-specific blog or website, particularly as Facebook is likely to get more use. A closed group on Facebook allows access to only those who have been invited to join. This means you can invite your class to the group and use it to share and discuss work privately. Remember that students need to be at least 13 years old to use Facebook.

Edmodo is a popular social networking site with an educational focus, which is free and works on all mobile devices. The teacher creates an account and sets up a space for each class; a specific entry code that the teacher controls restricts access to each space.

Try this — 'Show and tell' homework

Ask students to take a photo related to the current class topic. Begin the next lesson by asking them to share their photos with each other and to talk briefly about them (in pairs or small groups). Students can ask questions to find out more about the pictures. You can input language or use what the students say as the basis for further work. You could also record what they say (see Chapters 3 and 6) so that they can evaluate for themselves how well they did the task.

Try this — English around me

This awareness-raising activity encourages students to think about how much English is around them outside the classroom. Ask them to use their mobile devices to 'capture' English, for example on road or shop signs, advertising boards, etc. Ask them to share their photos via your closed group, and encourage students to comment on the photos as they would on a social networking site. You could also ask students to identify where English has been used incorrectly and get them to correct the mistakes. This will give them increased confidence in their language knowledge.

Why this works — Putting students behind the camera

Taking photos gives students the opportunity to connect the real world – their world – to the classroom. They can replace the predictable stock photos of the coursebook with images and contexts of their own choosing, which are relevant and meaningful to them. This fosters independence and creativity, thereby increasing learner motivation. Your lessons will come to life as you and your students learn about each others' interests, goals, and lives outside class.

Bringing coursebooks to life

There are many simple ways in which mobile learning can add interest to coursebook materials. Almost all topics and language points can be personalized by students taking their own photos or videos and bringing them into class to share. As shown earlier, students' photos can be used to practice a language area in a controlled yet personalized way; controlled in that students are working within the limited scope of the taught language point, and personalized through the use of their own photos. From a teaching point of view, this allows us to quickly see how well students have understood a language point.

Try this — **Key word challenge**

Set students a homework challenge (in teams or as individuals) to take photos representing all the key words covered in the lesson. In the next lesson, put students into groups to show their photos and see who found the most. Follow this up in the next lesson with a whole-class feedback session to clear up any issues, for example if a group doesn't think a photo is a valid representation of one of the words. You can also use the photos to revise meaning and pronunciation.

Why this works →

> **Consolidate learning**
>
> The process of reviewing key words, taking photos which represent them, then discussing their meaning in class is a valuable way for students to consolidate their learning.

Try this — **Scavenger hunts**

A scavenger hunt is an activity in which participants have to collect a number of objects chosen by the leader. The person or team that collects the most wins. You can adapt this so that 'collecting' the objects is done by taking a photo of them. Assign the class a different letter of the alphabet each week (for example, week 1 'A', week 2 'B', and so on). In teams or as individuals, students take photos of things from that week's unit(s) of the coursebook which begin with that letter. At the end of the week, ask students to share their photos, saying what the words are so that you can check pronunciation. Give points for each word found. At the end of the term, the student or team with the most points wins.

Try this — **Guess what's in my photo**

This is a variation of the popular game '20 Questions'. Put students into small groups. On their mobile device, one student in each group finds a photo that relates to the current coursebook topic. They keep it hidden from the rest of the group, who have a maximum of 20 yes/no questions to guess what the photo shows.

A further variation of this is 'Find the similarities'. Best played in pairs, students each find a photo, keep it hidden from their partner, and try to find five similarities between their photos by asking each other questions. For example: 'Are there people in the photo?' 'Is the sky blue?' Any fast finishers can be told to find more similarities.

A PHOTO TELLS A THOUSAND WORDS

Try this ☞ **Guess the phrasal verb**

After a coursebook presentation of phrasal verbs, put students into groups and give each group a set of phrasal verbs. Tell them to take photos contextualizing each of the phrasal verbs. The photos must also include one of the group members as proof that they didn't simply find their images online. You could set the actual photography as homework, after groups have discussed and planned what photos to take. In the next class, groups share their photos and try to guess each other's phrasal verbs. Students can use a collage maker app, which allows them to add text, to type in the phrasal verb. Share the photos via your closed group so that students have an illustrated set of phrasal verbs.
(With thanks to Laura Linzitto for this activity idea.)

Making more of photos

The activities suggested so far in this chapter for personalizing coursebook vocabulary and practising language points belong in the substitution and augmentation categories of the SAMR model. We will now move on to the modification category by looking at e-book creator apps. These allow you to create and share your own e-books. You can add photos, text, and audio, and the e-book can be saved as a PDF or in a format that is readable on different e-readers. The most well-known app is Book Creator. The full version isn't free, but students don't need to have the app on their devices, as they can produce the final e-book using your device.

Try this ☞ **Visual dictionaries**

Brainstorm the key features of books generally, then dictionaries specifically (for example, front cover, contents page, images, definitions), and tell students they are going to make their own English dictionary. Use your device to show an example of a dictionary entry. Then put students into small groups and give each group a portion of the words you want to cover, such as the vocabulary list at the back of the coursebook. Tell them they are going to write dictionary entries for each word. These should include the word, its definition, an example sentence, a photo, and an audio recording of the word together with the example sentence. Groups use their mobile devices to research their words, practise recording themselves (the final recording will be done in the e-book creator app), and take photos to provide context.

Ask them to send you their photos, then import one of the photos to each page of the e-book using the e-book creator app on your device. Tell students to type in their text (word, definition, and example sentence) and then record the audio. Students work together to design the front cover of their dictionary (for example, use a class photo and call it 'Shaun's Class's English Dictionary'). Add the front cover, then display the dictionary using a projector or mirroring. When you have reviewed the work with the students, you can share it so that all members of the class have a copy.

You can also use e-book creator apps for the following activities:
- Making a photo book: students add photos and a sentence about each one.
- Creating stories: students use the app to create their own stories (see Chapter 7).
- Presenting a topic: students research a topic (for example, my home town, favourite pet, etc.) and make an e-book to show what they discovered.

Why this works ⇒

> **Student-made materials**
> Making their own materials involves students working together to find their own real-world contexts for target words. By discussing, describing, practising, and recording their words, they make the vocabulary more meaningful and more memorable. Their finished work will give them a sense of pride and achievement – and also something tangible to show to their friends and family.

5 QR codes: a versatile classroom tool

QR codes appear on everything, from cereal packets to advertising boards at bus stops. Using the camera on their mobile device, students will discover how QR codes can enrich content, as they scan codes linked to websites, videos, and audio, etc., and how easy it is to share resources using these simple black-and-white squares. Students will also enjoy creating their own QR codes and sharing them with others, both inside and outside the classroom.

What is a QR code?

QR codes are two-dimensional barcodes containing information that can be read using a mobile device with a **QR reader** app. You can download a QR reader app for free from your app store, though bear in mind that the quality and functionality varies. If you want to use a free app, you might need to try out a few to find one you are comfortable with and can recommend to students. Using the camera on the mobile device, the QR reader scans the code, allowing you, for example, to read any text it contains or follow an internet link stored within the code.

One advantage of scanning a code to access a link is that it eliminates the need for students (or teachers) to spell it out. A wi-fi connection (or a SIM card) is needed for links to resources on the internet but not for offline content. You can use a **QR creator** app to easily generate your own QR codes for free, adding different types of information such as links to websites, text, audio, and videos.

Once you have downloaded a QR reader app on your mobile device, open it and scan the QR code in Figure 5.1, which should take you to a short text about QR codes. When scanning, make sure the code is centred in the middle of the screen. If you haven't read a QR code before, it may take a few attempts.

> Hello, this is an example of a QR code. You can put around 4,000 characters of text into this space. You can also give a link to a website or even add short audio clips.

FIGURE 5.1 *QR code*

Next, see how many QR codes you can find. If you go through food packaging and magazines, for example, you are likely to find at least one. Scan as many as you can to see what information they contain. You can try this activity with your students, in preparation for other activities using QR codes.

Try this **Surrounded by QR codes**

Ensure that students have all successfully downloaded a QR reader on their mobile devices. Before the lesson, set up an online noticeboard (see below). Ask students to take photos of QR codes outside class for homework and to post them on the online noticeboard. Recommend suitable categories (advertising, information, competitions, etc.) so that students only find appropriate content. The codes students capture should be shared with you first so that you can check in advance that all the content is suitable. In the next lesson, display the online noticeboard from your mobile device to show the codes. Then ask students to scan them and discuss in small groups which category each belongs to.

✓ Getting it right **Online noticeboards**

As the name suggests, these are online spaces that act like noticeboards. Unlike a physical class noticeboard, students can access online noticeboards anywhere, allowing them to add items both inside and outside the classroom. Popular noticeboard apps include Padlet, which works on all mobile devices, and Lino, for iOS and Android; both can also be accessed through a browser. Once you have created an account (which is free), you can create a noticeboard and share the link to it with the students. Anyone with access to the noticeboard can add text, images, video, or audio. You can set up as many noticeboards as you like for different uses and different classes.

Making and sharing QR codes

To make your own codes you need a QR creator app. Some apps can both read and create QR codes. There are also websites where you can create codes. With most QR creators, you begin by choosing what you want the code to contain; for example, a website link or text. You enter this information, then save or download the code. You can share your code electronically or print and display it as an image. We'll now explore the best ways of sharing codes with your students for the activities which follow.

QR CODES: A VERSATILE CLASSROOM TOOL

✓ Getting it right — Displaying QR codes

It's easy to print out your QR code for display. Simply open a blank document in a word processor app and add the QR code as an image, as well as any text you want to include. You can resize the QR code to make it bigger for display purposes. Finally, print out the finished item and put it on the wall.

Try this 👉 — Sharing codes

Open your noticeboard app and create a new noticeboard called 'Our favourite words'. Put an instruction on it asking students to visit the board after each lesson and to leave a note saying what their favourite word from the lesson was (leave a couple of words you liked as examples). Then share the board by clicking on the 'share' icon to find and copy the **URL**. Paste the URL into the 'create' area on your QR creator app and save or download the code that is created. Print out the saved code and put it on the classroom wall. At the end of class, ask students to scan the code to access the noticeboard. In the next lesson, use your mobile device to display the noticeboard and review the vocabulary.

✓ Getting it right — Ongoing revision

Keep the QR code on the wall so students can revisit the board and add words throughout the year. Return to the board regularly so that it serves as a virtual vocabulary box for class revision activities.

Classroom posters

QR codes can be included as part of presentations or research projects which link to extra information. You can also use them for games or language activities that get students out of their seats and using their mobile devices.

Try this 👉 — Ready-made practice

Search online for sites that give practice of a particular grammar point. Copy the URLs and make a QR code for each site, using your QR creator. Choose the 'URL' option, paste the links, and save your QR codes. Make a poster for each code and put them on your classroom wall. When students finish their coursebook exercises, invite them to scan the QR codes on the posters and do the additional exercises on their devices.

Creating your own content

So far we have explored using QR codes as a way to share links to online resources. As QR codes have the capacity to hold around 4,000 characters, you can also use them to create small reading texts or graded practice activities.

5 QR CODES: A VERSATILE CLASSROOM TOOL

Try this 👉 DIY practice

Use the 'text creator' option in your QR creator and choose 'text'. In the space provided, type the text you want to appear, and save the code. For a mixed-ability class, you could create different versions for the same language point. Figure 5.2 shows three examples for a lesson on modal verbs. The first exercise is a freer writing task for students who have understood the use of modal verbs. The second is for those who need practice which is a little more supported, while the third features the same sentences as the second but is for students who still need help with the meaning of the different modals.

1. Think of some rules that students should follow when using mobile devices in the classroom. Write down your ideas and then choose your two most important rules.

2. Complete the sentences with the correct modal verbs.
   1 You _____ switch off the sound on your phone before you come to class.
   2 Students _____ not use Facebook during lessons.
   3 You _____ not eat or drink near the school's tablets.
   4 You _____ never give your passwords to other people.
   5 We _____ keep apps up to date.

3. Choose the correct modal verbs to complete the sentences.
   1 You could / would / must switch off the sound on your phone before you come to class.
   2 Students must / would / will not use Facebook during lessons.
   3 You should / would / could not eat or drink near the school's tablets.
   4 You should / must / might never give your passwords to other people.
   5 We could / should / would keep apps up to date.

FIGURE 5.2   *QR code practice activities*

Why this works ▶ Discreet tasks

QR code posters conceal the level of the worksheet, so you can direct students to the poster which offers them the most appropriate support for their level.

Try this 👉 **QR answer keys**

Use QR codes to give answers to tasks. Choose the 'text' option in your QR creator and type the answers into the text box. Save the code, then either create a classroom poster or print out a copy. When students finish the task, invite them to scan the poster or the printed copy to check their answers. Alternatively, you can print the code onto stickers to put in students' books or on worksheets.

Why this works ⏩

> **Time savers**
>
> Self-checking answers encourages student independence. It also frees up valuable classroom time, which you can use to explore why students got things right or wrong.

QR code dictations

In Chapter 3 we looked at using text messaging for dictation as a way of increasing student motivation; QR codes can be used with the same effect.

Try this 👉 **Paired gap-fill dictation**

Find or create a suitable text and prepare two versions with different words removed. Select the 'text' option in the QR creator, paste the first gap-fill text, and create the QR code. Repeat for the second text. Create a classroom poster for each of the two QR codes, labelled A and B. In class, divide students into As and Bs. They scan the relevant QR code and take turns to dictate their texts to each other in A/B pairs. Both students note down the words that complete their gaps, then scan the other code to check their answers.

Try this 👉 **Running dictation**

Choose a suitable text and divide it into three or four parts. Select the 'text' option in your QR creator app, then either type or paste the first part into the space provided. Create and save the QR code. Repeat the process for each part of the text, then create a poster for each QR code. Divide students into groups of three or four. Tell the first person in the group to scan the first part of the text from the poster and dictate it for the group to write, either on their mobile device or on paper. The second student then scans the second part and dictates it to the group. This process continues until all parts have been scanned and dictated. When the group has finished, they can compare their texts to the QR code versions together.

Why this works ⏩

> **Taking the pressure off**
>
> In a traditional running dictation, students have to remember what they read. With the QR code version, students don't need to memorize the text, reducing stress levels and allowing them to focus more on the language itself.

> ✓ **Getting it right** **Copyright**
> Not everything on the internet is free to use. Be sure to check for any specific copyright restrictions before using a text.

QR code treasure hunts

You can use QR codes for class treasure hunts (or 'scavenger' hunts – see Chapter 4), where each clue leads to the location of the next one, with a reward or prize for the first person to reach the final location. On a smaller scale, the clues are simply numbered and put around the classroom for a timed activity or race. On a larger scale, you can place QR codes around the school. Treasure hunts are ideal for a class where not everyone has a smartphone or tablet, because only one QR reader is needed per group plus a second device for noting down the answers – although this can also be done with pen and paper.

> **Try this** 👉 **Treasure hunts for revision**
> Write ten true/false or multiple-choice questions to revise a particular topic or language point. In your QR creator, select the 'text' option and type the first question. Save the code. Repeat the process so that you have a QR code for each question, then print and display them around the classroom. In teams, students scan the codes and note down their answers. The first team to get all the correct answers wins.

> ✓ **Getting it right** **Making things easy**
> Using a QR creator to create each code for a treasure hunt can be time-consuming. A website called ClassTools allows you to enter all the information at once to generate the QR codes.

Student QR codes

So far the activities in this chapter have involved the teacher creating QR codes, but students can generate them, too. For example, if they have made a display about a coursebook topic, they can add QR codes that link to a variety of media to enhance the topic.

> **Try this** 👉 **Give students a voice**
> This activity works best alongside a display of student work that parents/carers and other students can see. Ask students to think of any information they could add to give interest to the display. Students work in pairs or small groups to prepare texts and record them on their devices. When they have finished, ask them to save their audio file with their initials in the file name so that it's clear who created it, then share it with you. Upload the files to the class website.

QR CODES: A VERSATILE CLASSROOM TOOL

To make the QR codes, tell students to copy the links to the audio, select the 'URL' option in the QR creator, and paste the link. Print out each saved QR code and place it next to the relevant piece of work. Parents/Carers and other students can then scan the QR code with their devices to access the audio.

Creating questionnaires and surveys

There are a number of websites that allow you to create surveys and questionnaires which are accessible on mobile devices. Perhaps the most well known is Google Forms, which is free to use but requires a Google account. Mobile devices can also be used for shorter polls and to get quick classroom responses. Websites and apps such as Kahoot!, Mentimeter, and Poll Everywhere allow teachers to create polls which students can answer using their mobile devices. Once a poll is created, you simply share a short URL (which the poll site creates) to it with the students.

With mobile devices and QR codes, students can create surveys to reach a wide audience; this should motivate them when preparing the survey and analysing the results. Moreover, surveys and questionnaires typically use large quantities of paper, so there is a clear advantage to creating and presenting them electronically. Apps such as Google Forms can also help to save you time when analysing and presenting the results. For example, creating a survey using Google Forms will generate a response spreadsheet which allows you and your students to see all the results in one place and can be used to present the data in the form of graphs and charts.

Try this **Creating and sharing a survey**

Tell students that they are going to create their own school-wide survey on a particular topic (food, pastimes, health, etc.). Ask them what questions are likely to be included in a survey on this topic. In groups, ask students to think of ten questions to include and to add them to the class chat group. Once all groups have added their questions, ask students as a class to decide if all the questions can be used (it is possible that some groups came up with similar questions, so the class needs to decide which ones to use). On your mobile device, go to a website for creating surveys, add the final set of questions, and create the survey. Copy the URL, send it to students via the chat group, and ask them to complete the survey on their devices.

After the lesson, create a new QR code. Select the 'URL' option in the QR creator and paste the link to the survey. Save or download the QR code, then print it out, add it to a public noticeboard in the school, and invite people to take the survey. In the next lesson, share the results of the survey with the class by projecting the answers from your mobile device. Ask students to discuss the results and write a summary. They can create a QR code of their summaries to display on the noticeboard so that everyone can see the results of the survey.

Try this **An instant poll**

Choose a lesson in the coursebook which has questions asking for students' opinions and responses. For example:
- Would you like to learn another language?

53

- How often do you eat out?
- Which of these news topics interests you most?

Before the lesson, create a poll on your mobile device using a polling app. Type in a question with the answer choices and save the poll, then create a QR code with a link to it. In class, share the QR code with the students and ask them to respond to the poll using their mobile device. Allow a few seconds for everyone to vote, then project the results to find out what the class thinks.

Why this works ➡

> **What do students think?**
>
> Instant polling gives you a snapshot of students' opinions. Everyone can take part; and since polls are anonymous, students can answer truthfully without worrying what others think. You can encourage independent work by asking students to create and share their own polls. The use of polls isn't limited to questions from the coursebook. They can also be used to gauge the students' understanding and get feedback, by using polls as a form of exit ticket (see Chapter 10).

Putting it all together

QR codes are often used on tourist sites and in museums to allow visitors to access more information about the place or exhibits. You can use this idea for a classroom project, combining the use of internet links, text, and audio.

Try this ☞ **A tour of the school**

Tell students they are going to create a tour of the school by displaying QR codes at key locations. The codes will contain relevant information at each location (for example, school history at the school entrance, information about the staff at the school office, etc.). Create an online noticeboard for students to use to collaborate and share their ideas. Students start by deciding which locations to include in the tour and which media to use for each presentation. Once students have come up with ideas, the class should agree on a final list of locations. Put the class into three groups and divide the locations between them. Each group plans what to do for their location(s) (for example, taking photos, interviewing and recording staff to obtain biographical information, etc.).

In the next lesson, students prepare their presentations and upload them to the class website so that each group can provide you with a link that can be shared as a QR code. Paste each URL into your QR creator app one by one and create the codes. Print them out and ask students to display them at the relevant locations. They should use their mobile devices to take the tour themselves to check that it's ready for others to experience.

Why this works ▶ **The convenience of the QR code**

QR codes are versatile, and they can help to save valuable classroom time. Once created, a code lasts until it is deleted, so it can be used repeatedly. They are easy to make and can hold or instantly link to most types of media, ensuring that students go directly to the correct website without the risk of incorrectly copying URLs. Using them on classroom posters allows you to provide a motivating range of extra tasks for students.

6 Audio recording

The development of audio recording apps has made it easy for students to record themselves and share the recordings using their mobile devices. This can bring many benefits to language learning. For example, by listening to students' recordings, teachers are better able to identify their individual needs and to feed back accordingly. Students can also peer-review or self-review their work and build up a portfolio of authentic listening material to share with teachers and parents/carers.

Voice recognition

Voice recognition is a feature that is available on most mobile devices – for example, Siri on Apple, Cortana on Windows, Voice Search on Google – and it can be an entertaining way to practise language.

Try this **Ask a question**

Asking a question to the mobile device introduces students to voice recognition while at the same time practising questions and their pronunciation. Ask students to change the voice recognition language setting on their device to English. Model the activity by asking your device a question. For example: *What is the meaning of life?* Students then think of their own questions, ask their devices, and see what answers they get. Ask students which answers they found most interesting or amusing.

✓ Getting it right **Short and sweet**

Keep this activity short, and be on hand to help. Voice recognition technology is by no means perfect, and questions are often reformulated even when you ask them correctly. If this happens too often, students may become frustrated. Moreover, questions are often answered with a link to a website which might be overwhelming (and therefore demotivating) for lower-level students, so make sure to support those who need help.

Why this works **Say it right**

Using voice recognition can be valuable pronunciation practice, because students have to say things correctly and coherently for their device to recognize the question and provide an answer. If their question is misunderstood, students will need to improve their pronunciation or reformulate the question and try again. This amounts to a useful drilling-like exercise where students are encouraged to think about and assess their own language production.

AUDIO RECORDING

Try this · **Take a note**

Before the lesson, make a list of words recently covered in class that you want students to practise pronouncing. Make sure they have changed their device's voice recognition language setting to English. Then demonstrate asking your device to 'take a note'. Once the device responds, say some of the words you want to practise. Point out that as you speak, the words appear on screen, and that any words you mispronounce will be typed incorrectly. Deliberately mispronouncing a few of the words will illustrate this. Write the list of target vocabulary on the board, then have your students use voice recognition to practise saying the words. If they make a mistake, they should repeat the words they mispronounced and keep practising until they get them right.

Try this · **Tongue twisters**

Search online for tongue twisters containing sounds that students have difficulty with. For example, if they have trouble with /v/ and /w/, search for 'V and W tongue twisters'. Send the class a tongue twister via your messaging app and ask students to practise saying it to each other. Then ask them to check their pronunciation using voice recognition on their device to see if the tongue twister appears correctly on-screen. As a follow up, students can record the tongue twister on the messaging app (by tapping on the microphone icon). They can re-record until they are happy with their recording, then share it with the class. Once all the messages have been shared, give students feedback. If students enjoy competition, decide as a class who recited the tongue twister best.

Why this works · **Visual pronunciation**

Students can find pronunciation difficult because they don't know how they are mispronouncing a word or phrase. By turning speech to text, voice recognition can make it possible for students to see their mistakes.

Try this · **Sound selfies**

If students are struggling to produce a particular sound, ask them to take selfies as they focus on their mouth shape – for example, the tight 'o' shape at the end of the diphthong sound /əʊ/ (you can demonstrate how to do this). Once they feel they are able to make the sound correctly, they can check using voice recognition. Sound selfies provide students with a way of checking that they are producing sounds correctly, and they can also be used as a point of reference for future self-study, reminding them how to make the sounds.

Making recordings

As well as being useful for practising and checking pronunciation, a mobile device is an excellent tool for making longer recordings. We have already looked at this briefly in Chapter 3, specifically in relation to using audio recording as a means of self-assessment, and in Chapter 5 with QR codes (see page 52). Here we'll look at a broader range of activities which involve using audio recording to practise and assess language use.

6 AUDIO RECORDING

Which app?

If your mobile device doesn't already have an audio recording app installed, you'll need to download one. Ideally you want a recording app that is easy to use, i.e. where you just press a button to start recording. More importantly, you want an app that saves the recording in a common format such as MP3, which makes it easier to manipulate and share. Use the following questions to help you decide what you want from an audio recording app:

- What are you going to record?
- How will students listen to recordings?
- Will you be publishing them?
- Are you going to make podcasts?

✓ Getting it right — Upload to the cloud

Audio files are often too large to email from a mobile device, so it's useful to have an app that automatically uploads the audio file to your cloud storage, or one which has its own storage space where the file will be easily accessible to students. AudioBoom and Spreaker are free to use, though they limit recording length and require you to create an account.

Try this 👉 What's that sound?

Capture a sound outside class, such as traffic, construction work, or a street market; the more interesting and unusual the sound, the better. You could choose a sound that relates to a coursebook topic or simply one to use in a warm-up exercise. Open your chosen audio recording app, press 'record' and capture a few seconds of the sound, then save the recording. In class, play the sound and ask students to guess what it is. Ask the student who guesses correctly to record a sound for the next lesson, and repeat the process. Alternatively, use your sound as an example, then ask all students to record sounds for the next lesson. In that lesson, put the students into small groups to guess the sounds.

Why this works ▶ An ongoing game

This is a short engaging activity which you can use each week to link class activities with the outside world. Giving students the task of finding interesting sounds will motivate them and help to create a positive class dynamic. You can also use this as an opportunity to practise language points, such as yes/no questions to work out the sound (for example, 'Is it in the street?') or modal verbs of deduction (for example, 'It might be a car.').

Try this 👉 Off-site interviews

Ask students to prepare an interview. For a coursebook unit on the family, for example, they could interview a family member. In pairs or small groups, they discuss and agree on a list of questions, then record their interviews for homework. In the next lesson, students play their recordings to the rest of the class and ask each other questions.

AUDIO RECORDING

✓ Getting it right — **OK to use the first language**

If interviewees (for example, family members) don't speak English, ask students to first say the question in English and then in their first language. When the interviewee answers in their first language, students should follow with an English translation. Students might need to pause the recording while they think of the translation.

Assessment

With a large class, it can be difficult to listen to everyone and give feedback for speaking activities. Individual recordings of students allow you to assess everyone's performance.

Try this — **Audio homework**

When you have finished a speaking activity in class, have a feedback session to discuss what students did well and how they could improve. For homework, ask students to do the task again and to record themselves using their mobile device. They can do the task as many times as they like until they are happy with their recording. They should then save the recording and send it to you by email or upload it to a cloud-sharing site. Listen to the recordings and evaluate them. You can record your evaluations and send them back to the students to listen to.

✓ Getting it right — **Dealing with recorded homework**

You are likely to receive recorded homework at different times. Make it clear to students how you will deal with their work and when they can expect to receive feedback. Having a clear procedure should ensure that the process runs smoothly.

Why this works — **The benefit of audio feedback**

Audio feedback allows students to hear how words and phrases should be pronounced; and you can inject enthusiasm into your feedback, which is harder to do effectively in written form. If used regularly, you can create a recorded portfolio of students' work that can be used to track their progress.

Try this — **Recycling coursebook material**

At the end of a coursebook unit, divide the class into three groups. Assign each group one of the following areas to work on: 1) grammar, 2) vocabulary, 3) topic. Tell students they are going to produce audio exercises for their area, which will be used to revise the unit.

Group 1: Create gap-fill exercises to practise key grammar.
Group 2: Create definitions and gapped example sentences for key vocabulary.
Group 3: Create true/false statements about key themes in the coursebook unit.

(Note: Students should use a sound such as a beep to mark any gaps.)

6   AUDIO RECORDING

When each group is ready, ask them to record their exercises and answer keys, then upload them to your group site so they can be shared with the class (recordings can also be put on a class blog or website so they can be accessed again by the students). Students listen and complete each other's activities and check their answers.

Why this works ▶ **Audio revision**

Asking students to record rather than write adds variety to familiar tasks; and in SAMR terms, we are augmenting by adding the skills of speaking and listening. It also creates material that the students can go back and listen to in the future.

✓ Getting it right **Recording quality**

Mobile devices have sensitive microphones which will pick up background noise if students are all recording at the same time. If possible, use empty classrooms or corridor space to allow students to spread out.

Rehearsals will give students the opportunity to work out where they need to sit in relation to the microphone; they should speak towards it, holding the device close to their mouth if necessary. This will help to make them sound more natural if they are reading from their notes.

Podcasting

A **podcast** is a digital recording that you can download from the internet and play on your mobile device or computer. It's a popular way of listening to audio content (often by subscription to a series of episodes) that you can access anywhere, pausing or repeating sections as often as you like. Podcasts could be recordings of radio programmes, lectures, interviews, textbook materials, music, poetry, vocabulary, novels – there is really no limit to what's available. Podcasts are a great way to bring authentic listening material to students, about areas that interest them or to update or enliven a coursebook topic. If this doesn't appeal to your students, make your own – or get the students to do so.

Try this ☞ **What should we listen to?**

Ask students what they listen to on their devices besides music, and how they decide what to listen to. Make a list on the board to use as the criteria for what the class will choose to listen to. Next, ask students to go to a website or app that offers podcasts for download, such as iTunes, Stitcher, or PodOmatic. Tell them to each choose a podcast for the class to listen to and give them a few minutes to look through the sites. (Remind them that they can listen to samples of the podcasts or play part of an episode.)

AUDIO RECORDING

Put students into small groups to share their choices and say why they chose them. Each group should then choose one of the podcasts to add to a shortlist for the class to use to decide which podcast to listen to. Play it to the whole class (or have students listen individually using headphones). Discuss together whether it was a good choice, and ask the students if they would listen to another episode of the podcast, if it is available.

Getting it right — **Choosing the right podcast**

If you are going to listen to podcasts in class, choose (or encourage students to choose) ones that can lead to post-listening discussions. These include audio dramas and documentary-style podcasts such as those that discuss real-life mysteries.

Why this works — **Introducing podcasts**

This activity highlights the range of podcasts available. While you might not want to dedicate time to podcasts in class, giving students the tools to decide what to listen to should encourage them to listen to authentic material outside class.

Making a podcast

You can make a podcast quite easily and professionally on a mobile device; the apps mentioned on page 58 will get you started. For even more professional results, you could consider more powerful recording apps such as GarageBand and bossjock studio (available for iOS). These allow you to edit and merge many different audio recordings. Find out what else students listen to online, such as game reviews, fashion tips, etc. and use these ideas to inform what types of podcast you make with them.

Try this — **The teacher's voice**

Create your own mini-podcasts for specific language points. For example, record yourself giving grammar presentations with some examples and even translation. Save your recording and make it available on the class website for the students to download.

Why this works — **Mini podcasts**

These can act as reminders and additional support for students when doing homework or studying for a test. They can also be used as part of a flipped learning approach (see Chapter 10).

Try this — **Creating a class podcast**

Tell students they are going to record a radio show for the school. Put them into groups to brainstorm what kinds of segments they want to include; for example, reviews (of apps, games, films, music, etc.), interviews (with students or teachers), school news, or audio stories. Agree as a class what to include.

Allocate segments to different groups and ask them to discuss ideas for content. Monitor the discussions, providing language input and advice as needed. After groups have rehearsed their segments, have a class run-through so that students can decide on the best order in which to record the segments.

Schedule a recording day as a deadline for preparation. Groups now record and save their segments. If you are using an app that brings together several recordings, ask each group to send you their recorded segment. Play the podcast to the class, making sure the upload settings are on 'public' so that it can be shared and added to the class (or school) website.

✓ Getting it right

'I don't want to be recorded'

Remember that you need students' permission if you are going to make a podcast publicly available. If any students don't want to be recorded, give them the role of director or producer so that they are still involved.

Why this works ▶

Class podcasts

Making a class podcast is a project that engages students both inside and outside class, and which can be done over a series of lessons. It can also be the focus of a project for an English club. By creating audio material, students practise their speaking skills, and the audience gets listening practice. Class podcasts involve planning and rehearsing, so students have the opportunity to put into practice the language they have learned and focus on saying it correctly. If the idea seems too ambitious to do as a first project, you can use the separate segments to make mini podcasts, with each student recording their own short review of a book, film, game, or piece of music.

Part 3: Mobile devices: projects and beyond

7 Digital storytelling

Storytelling is a tradition that goes back through human history; most of us enjoy a story in one form or another, whether it's a film, a book, or something somebody has told us. Storytelling is also a popular tool in language learning, because it is engaging for students and also practises key literacy skills.

Why digital storytelling?

Digital storytelling means, as the name suggests, telling stories in electronic form, combining different digital media. These might include text, audio, images (photos, screenshots, etc.), or video. Digital storytelling presents new opportunities for creating and learning, as students have the freedom to express themselves through different combinations of digital media using their mobile devices. For example, they could make a simple photo story, a more complex video story, or even a stop-motion animation.

Digital storytelling brings a number of advantages for language learning, not least the fact that creating stories is an effective way of practising and consolidating language. Storytelling makes use of many aspects of language, from narrative tenses through to adverbs of manner and direct and reported speech. You can use digital stories to focus the students' attention on one language area or give them the freedom to choose whatever language they like and use it to assess their level.

Another key advantage of digital storytelling is its ability to increase engagement, by giving students the chance to work together on a project to achieve a clear outcome and the space to develop their ideas while learning from each other. As their teacher, you can stand by to offer help, advice, and support when necessary so that they are able to successfully express their ideas. The following is a useful warm-up activity.

Try this → **Photo stories**

Put students into small groups and ask each student to find a photo on their mobile device that they are happy to share with their group; the photo might be of a person, a place, or an object. Then ask them to line up their devices so that the photos are displayed in a row. Tell them that this is the order of events in a story that begins 'Last weekend …'. Now tell each group to make up a story that includes all the photos (they don't need to write it down at this point). Remind them that they will need to use the past tense. While they are planning their stories, give them some help but not too much. When they are ready to tell their

DIGITAL STORYTELLING

stories, one student in each group should open the audio recording app on their mobile device to record the story. Students then listen to the recording and identify ways to improve it. Once they have made their improvements, each group should play their story to the rest of the class.

Storytelling apps

There are many storytelling apps, and some can be accessed on the internet. These apps have a variety of features that students can utilize for creative projects; for example, using their own voice to narrate the story, or incorporating different pictures and backgrounds. As a starting point, try Adobe Spark for iOS or PhotoVoice for Android. Story Cubes and Story Dice provide prompts for story writing, and Story Wheel has prompts specifically for fairy tales. PhotoVoice, along with other popular apps, allows students to combine images with their voice and text to create audiovisual stories. (Search for 'photo and voice apps' in your app store for others.)

✓ Getting it right — Do some research

Before you use a storytelling app in class, research what will work well for your class. Use the guidelines in Chapter 2 for choosing apps to consider how much time the app lets you record for and how easy it is to save and share files.

Try this — My journey to school

For homework, ask students to take five photos illustrating their journey to and from school. You will need to do this yourself before the next lesson and use your chosen storytelling app to create an example. You can use your example to highlight any specific language you want students to use, such as descriptive adjectives, present or past tenses, etc.

In the next lesson, show students your photos and briefly explain each one in the context of your journey. Ask students to work in pairs to show each other their photos and talk about their own journeys. This will serve as a rehearsal before they record their stories. Next, ask students to open the app they are using to record the story. Tell them to start a new story and upload their first photo. They should add some text to explain what the photo shows and how it relates to their journey. If possible, they should also record their text. Tell them to repeat the process for all five photos. Finally, they should give their story a title and share it with you, either by sending a link or uploading it to the cloud. In groups, students then read and listen to their stories in turn and ask questions about them. Finally, bring the class together to discuss what they found most interesting about the different stories.

Planning a digital story

As with any good story, an effective digital story requires planning. You need to decide what type of story you want students to create (for example, a personal account, a documentary, a fantasy). This will help to determine the length of research time, what images students need and how to source them, what apps are appropriate, and so on. You then need to consider how much time students are going to invest in the story, both in and out of class.

✓ *Getting it right*

> **Digital story checklist**
> Use the checklist below to help prepare your first digital storytelling lesson. When you can answer all the questions, you are ready to begin.
> 1. What is the target language and the overall learning outcome?
> 2. What is the right length for the story (how many words, how many pictures), and how long will it take to make?
> 3. What technology will students use? Do their mobile devices support the apps I want to use? Is there any cost involved?
> 4. Do I have an example of a digital story I can show students?
> 5. How will the final story be shared (for example, in a group screening, on a group site)?

The key elements of digital storytelling

Stories provoke different reactions in different people, so what one person thinks is good may not get a positive reaction from someone else. Nevertheless, it is important that students understand the role of the key elements of digital storytelling so that they can make their own evaluations.

Plot: What happens and where? Make sure that students are clear about the separate events that make up the story, the order in which they happen, and where they take place.

Pace: A good story doesn't move too slowly or too quickly and gives the audience time to understand it. The amount of photos, video, and audio can affect pace, so they should be used with this in mind.

Soundtrack: This could be music or a voiceover. Any music should be appropriate to the mood of the story.

Characters: Who is the story about, and who are the most important people in it?

Themes: What aspects of the story will keep the audience interested? For example, will the 'hero' face great difficulties, and will he eventually win? How do the characters feel at key points in the story, and do their feelings change as the story progresses?

DIGITAL STORYTELLING

Try this 👉 **What makes a good digital story?**

Prepare small texts that explain the key elements of storytelling described on page 66. Turn your texts into QR codes (see Chapter 5) and put them around the classroom. Next, find an example of a digital story that is suitable for your class (try searching for 'digital story examples' on YouTube). At the start of the lesson, put the key elements of storytelling on the board and tell students that they are important components of a good story. Ask them to discuss in small groups what each one means, then check their ideas by scanning the QR codes. Check that everyone has understood the meaning of all the elements. Finally, show students your digital story and ask them to discuss how good it is in terms of each of the key elements.

The planning process

To plan effectively, it is useful to map out the process of creating a digital story from start to finish. An example process is shown in Figure 7.1.

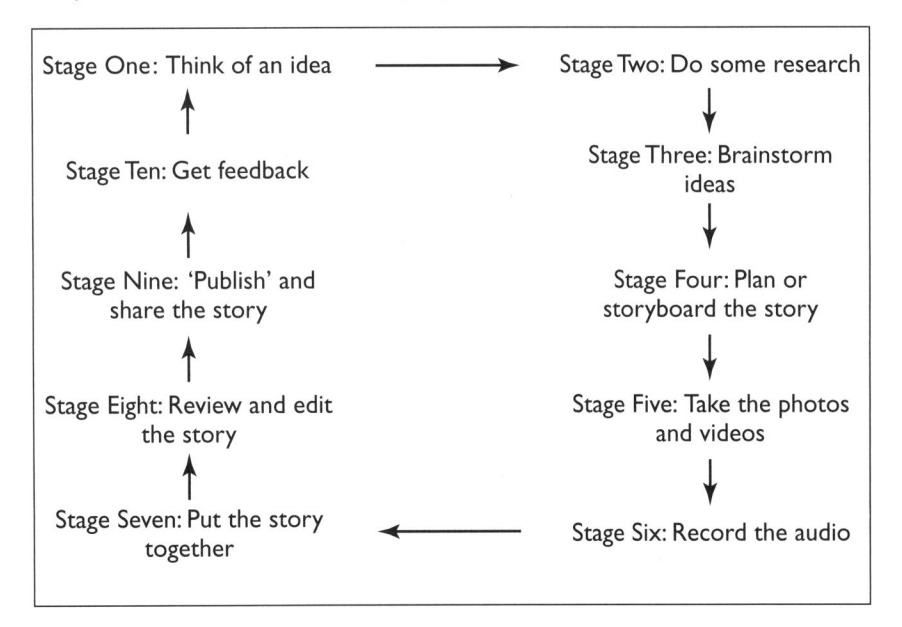

```
Stage One: Think of an idea  ─────▶  Stage Two: Do some research
         ▲                                      │
         │                                      ▼
Stage Ten: Get feedback              Stage Three: Brainstorm ideas
         ▲                                      │
         │                                      ▼
Stage Nine: 'Publish' and            Stage Four: Plan or
share the story                      storyboard the story
         ▲                                      │
         │                                      ▼
Stage Eight: Review and edit         Stage Five: Take the photos
the story                            and videos
         ▲                                      │
         │                                      ▼
Stage Seven: Put the story  ◀─────  Stage Six: Record the audio
together
```

FIGURE 7.1   *Planning a digital story*

While at first glance the diagram in Figure 7.1 might make the process seem rather complicated, it provides a useful reminder of the steps involved in creating a story and illustrates how best to maximize both the language learning opportunities and the effectiveness of the project. Not everything has to be done in class; for example, stages two, five, and six could be set as homework. You may even choose to make this a longer-term project, with students working on it in small chunks over a number of lessons. Flexibility is important to ensure that students remain motivated to complete the project.

Try this 👉 **Planning a story**

Divide students into groups to do stage one from Figure 7.1. For younger students, give them a theme, such as a story about a monster or an adventure at the seaside. For older students, give them time to think of an idea; if they can't think of one, give them suggestions of things to include in the story, such

DIGITAL STORYTELLING

as a stolen phone or a camping trip. For stages two and three, allow time for the groups to work together on developing the key elements of their story (see page 66); this will maximize language production as they discuss and shape the story. For stage four, give each group a handout such as the one in Figure 7.2 (the examples are based on the story of *Little Red Riding Hood*). Remind students to pay attention to the key elements when filling in the details of their story. This will help them decide what to include and how each part contributes to the overall story. Provide help and advice as they create their storyboards.

Story title: *Little Red Riding Hood*				
Students:				
	Description of photo	Plot summary	What will you write or say?	Soundtrack
1	Little Red Riding Hood with a basket talking to her mum.	LRRH is setting out on her journey through the woods to take food to her grandma's house.	LRRH's mum: Walk fast through the woods and don't talk to strangers!	Upbeat music to represent LRRH's lively mood as she sets out on her journey.
2				
3				
4				
5				

FIGURE 7.2   *Creating a storyboard*

Trailers as digital stories

A trailer is a short video used to advertise a film. You can use the concept of a trailer to create a digital story on a mobile device.

On all Apple mobile devices, you can download Apple's iMovie. This is a powerful video-editing app which provides templates you can use to turn your own photos and videos into films. The app includes a function called 'trailers', which provides generic trailer templates for many genres of film. The template acts as a storyboard to guide the user in choosing media to create a short film trailer. If no one in your class has an Apple device, an alternative would be to use an app such as VideoShow or Movie Maker.

Making trailers is time-consuming, although it can be done in one lesson provided you keep to strict deadlines. One way to break up the work is to use one lesson for planning, get students to take any photos or videos they need as homework, and create and show the trailer in a second lesson.

Try this   **Create a school trailer**

Lesson one: Before class, find two or three trailers of different genres online that you can show in class. Ask students what the last film they saw was, which upcoming ones they are excited about, and how they decide which films to watch. Introduce the idea of trailers before showing the ones you chose (either project the trailers from your device or share links to them). Ask students to discuss what genre of film each trailer shows (action, romance, comedy, etc.). Then put students into groups to discuss what genre would work best for a film about the school.

Projecting or mirroring your mobile device, show the class the trailer templates in your video-editing app and tell them they are going to create a trailer that will act as an 'advert' for their school. Give the groups time to plan their trailer, making sure they refer to the template as a guide for what they need to include, and be on hand to help them. By the end of this lesson, they should know what photos and videos they need to take before the next lesson.

Lesson two: Working in the same groups, students transfer the photos and videos to the device being used to make the trailer. Next, they open the video-editing app and import the photos and videos into the appropriate place in their chosen trailer template. When all the media and any text required have been added, students should check their trailer to make sure they are happy with the final result. Once all groups are ready, turn down the lights and play the trailers.

Assessing students' digital stories

While it might be tempting to approach the assessment of a digital story as an exercise in language correction, it is perhaps fairer to assess it in terms of what has been produced. If you asked students to produce a trailer, did they achieve this? If we assess language and ignore the creative form, we may demotivate students and make them less likely to engage with future projects. We would also be ignoring the real-life purpose of the created work. In order to avoid this, teachers who regularly create digital stories with their students favour using rubrics. The added advantage of using such a system is that it can also be used for peer assessment.

What are rubrics?

Rubrics can be used to set out the criteria for a particular task – that is, what students are expected to produce. They can also serve as a marking scale for assessing work. Rubrics can be used for many productive tasks and are perhaps the most common tool for assessing digital stories. (See *Useful apps and websites* for a number of examples on the internet which are free to use.)

When creating a rubric for a digital story, a good place to start is with the key elements discussed on page 66. You can assign a description and a points scale to each element and add additional categories for language areas such as vocabulary and grammar. An example is provided in Figure 7.3.

7   DIGITAL STORYTELLING

Digital Story Assessment			
Name of group/students:			
Name of project:			
Points awarded:			
Story element	3 points	2 points	1 point
1 Plot	We completely understand what happens.	We understand most of what happens.	It is difficult to understand what happens.
2 Pace	The pacing is good and helps the audience get involved.	The pacing is good and helps the audience gets involved. However, sometimes the story moves too fast/too slowly.	The pacing is not good for the style of story. The story is told too fast or too slowly, which makes it difficult to follow.
3 Soundtrack	The music and voices add the right emotion to the story.	Most of the time, the music and voices add the right emotion to the story.	The music is badly chosen and does not fit well with the story.
4 Characters	We know who all the characters are and why they are in the story.	We know who all the characters are, but are not always sure why they are in the story.	It is difficult to understand who the characters are or why they are in the story.
5 Themes	The themes are easy to understand.	The themes can be understood but are not always clear.	It is difficult to understand what the themes are.

FIGURE 7.3   *Rubric for assessing a digital story*

Try this   **Peer-assessing a digital story**

Before the lesson, decide on the rubric that you want students to use. Make enough copies so that every group has one for each story; if there are five groups and five stories, you will need four copies of the rubric for each group – assuming groups do not assess their own story.

After the groups have presented their stories, ask them to assess the stories by deciding how many points to give for each key element. They can add up the points for each story to give an overall assessment score. When all the stories have been assessed, each group receives all the scores for their story. They can review these, asking other groups for clarification of the points they gave if necessary. If there is time, the groups can use the assessments to edit their work.

Why this works ➡ | **Peer assessment**
As long as students have been provided with clear guidelines and the appropriate language for giving feedback, peer assessment can give them a better understanding of a task and the processes involved. It encourages students to analyse their own performance, as well as that of others, which can improve the way they approach the task, and therefore benefit language production.

Why this works ➡ | **The benefits of digital storytelling**
Digital storytelling expands upon and enriches traditional storytelling. Equipped simply with their mobile devices, students are able to create multimedia stories which can include video, audio, and photos, as well as text. Making stories lends itself to being a collaborative task where students can direct their own learning – practising their planning and multimedia skills, as well as developing their potential for creativity. Finally, using a mobile device allows students to share their stories with a wider audience than they might have reached otherwise, through film screenings or by publishing the stories online.

8 Video and animation

We are living in an era of the online video. Every minute, hundreds of hours of video are uploaded to YouTube, and young people spend on average 12 hours a week watching online videos. Increased mobile device ownership is clearly a contributing factor to this development, as is the fact that many mobile devices have video-recording capability. Depending on their device, students can take standard video, time-lapse video, or even slow-motion video, both in and out of class.

No longer dependent on the school having expensive video equipment, teachers can use mobile devices to capture moments of learning, add variation to an activity, and engage students in collaborative projects. Once a video clip has been recorded, a mobile device allows for easy editing, playback, and sharing. Video can be used as a way of bringing dialogues and role-plays to life; and, as with audio recording, it enables students to evaluate their language performance.

First, choose a suitable dialogue. A quick look through your coursebook should provide various possibilities, from ready-made dialogues to reading texts or pronunciation activities. You can also follow up a listening activity by using the audioscript.

Try this **Recording a dialogue**

Put students into small groups and ask them to create a realistic video of a coursebook dialogue. The students in each group decide on their roles, including actors, a camera operator, and a director (you can add other roles as necessary, such as a set designer responsible for finding or making props). Give groups time to prepare and rehearse before recording their videos. Watch them as a whole-class activity and ask students to vote on who they think made the most realistic video.

Why this works **Coursebook video**

Using the coursebook is a simple way of introducing students to recording video on their mobile devices. Turning coursebook dialogues into video is more engaging than simply reading them aloud, and the language focus should be more memorable. Planning and organizing a coursebook video provides additional practice and extension of the language. Students are also likely to enjoy watching and assessing their work at the end. Recording the process gives the teacher an opportunity to revisit common language errors with students at a later stage.

Short-form video

Short-form videos are often referred to as 'snackable content' – web material that's easy to access and share. Snackable video content has a limited length (similar to the limited number of characters in an SMS text message). Apps such as Instagram and Snapchat, which have helped to popularize the snackable video form, are easy to use; you simply point and shoot. Initially, you could even just use the camera on your mobile device to make a short video clip. For example, instead of taking a photo of a phrasal verb (see Chapter 4), you could capture a short video to contextualize it.

Why this works ▶

> **Focusing the mind**
>
> Imposing a limit on the length of video makes students think carefully about the content and is a motivating way of encouraging critical thinking skills such as planning.

Try this 👉 **Tell a story in 30 seconds**

This activity introduces students to the concept of short-form video. Ask students to discuss the following question in pairs or small groups and take notes: 'If you only had 30 seconds to tell a story, what story would you tell?' Groups take turns to tell the class their ideas, and the other groups ask questions and give feedback so the ideas can be improved. Next, students create a video of their story. Give them time to plan (see Chapter 7), and remind them that it should be only 30 seconds long. Depending on the time available, students may need to continue the activity as homework. In the next lesson, they show their videos and the class decides who created the best story.

Try this 👉 **Making a how-to video**

Giving instructions for how to do something features in many coursebooks and is often the focus of exam writing tasks. Following a lesson on giving instructions, ask students to capture a short how-to video on their mobile device for homework, illustrating what they learned in class; for example, 'How to boil an egg' or 'How to take and edit a photo'. In the next lesson, ask students to work together to create verbal instructions for the videos. As a variation or extension, ask students to post their videos on the class website or blog. Other students can then write up the instructions under the video.

Why this works ▶

> **Bringing instructions to life**
>
> Giving students the freedom to create a set of instructions that are meaningful to them, and to possibly star in the video themselves, makes the task more motivating. Because how-to videos mirror real life, they add authenticity to the task and the language used. And including instructions provides a way of checking that students have understood the key language required.

Creating longer videos

So far in this chapter, we have looked at short video activities limited in length and the language used. Now we will look at making longer videos. To inspire students and generate ideas, ask them to watch short films that have been entered in competitions; for example, search on the BBC website or YouTube for the short film competition Well Done U.

✓ Getting it right | **Inappropriate content**

Whenever you direct students to an internet site, be aware that some of the content might be inappropriate. One way around this is to go to the site before the lesson, note appropriate URLs, and give these to your students to choose from.

Try this ☞ | **Daily routines**

Lesson one: In preparation for students to make their own videos, search online for videos illustrating daily routines, or make one of your own. Play the video to the class and use it to highlight and elicit vocabulary for typical daily activities. For homework, ask students to use their mobile device to make a video showing their daily routine.

Lesson two: Put students into pairs to share their videos, and tell them to note down what their partner did in their video. After watching, ask them to find out how often their partner does a particular activity by asking questions; for example, 'Do you usually get up at 7 a.m.?', 'Do you always have salad for lunch?'. They should add the answers to their notes. Once their notes are complete, ask them to write a voiceover commentary for their partner's video. They can either record the audio over the video or simply speak as the video plays. Share the completed videos and commentaries with the whole class, and ask students to decide how similar their daily routines are.

✓ Getting it right | **Combining video clips**

When recording their daily routine, students are likely to take a number of short clips. To combine them into one continuous video, they will need to use an additional video-editing app. Popular ones for iOS include iMovie, Splice, and Quik (which is also available for Android). Another Android app is Magisto; and for Windows there's Movie Maker. Alternatively, enter a phrase such as 'free video editor for mobile device' in a search engine and see what comes up.

Avatars

Computer and mobile games often use an **avatar** – a graphic image of a character – to represent the player. On mobile devices, avatars have the ability to record speech, turn text into speech, and even express some emotions through facial and physical gestures. These functions make avatars an excellent tool for language practice.

If your students already know each other, it can be difficult to motivate them to practise language for sharing basic personal information. Using avatars can introduce a fresh and fun alternative. The following activity uses the app Voki for Education (available for both iOS and Android), which also has a website for anyone without a compatible device. Voki for Education offers a selection of many types of avatar and is easy to use. Other avatar apps include Tellagami and WeeMee Avatar Creator.

Try this **Introductions**

Ask students to design an avatar using your chosen app and get them to record a short introductory message, which should include a name and some basic facts about the avatar (age, hobbies, etc.). Students can then share their avatars by sending links to each other. Once they have been shared, students work in small groups to talk about why they created that particular avatar. If you are new to the class, ask students to create an avatar that represents them. Their recorded message should include real facts about themselves that the students want to share with you and their classmates.

✓ Getting it right **Teaching an avatar to speak**

There are usually two ways to give an avatar a voice: you can either record yourself speaking or type in the words you want the avatar to say. Many avatar apps use basic software to turn text into speech. While the speech produced is mostly accurate, the avatars can sometimes struggle with vowel sounds and certain letter combinations. Encourage students to check the speech before they finalize their avatar's message. If the avatar says a word incorrectly, tell students to spell it phonetically, as this can often achieve more accurate pronunciation. Monitor students to help and advise them.

Try this **Guessing games with avatars**

Avatars work well for guessing games. Students don't need to create a new avatar for each game, as they can simply edit and change the message. For the following three games, students give their avatar a message to share with other students, who respond with their guess.

Guess the word
After a vocabulary lesson, students have their avatar share the definition of a word or phrase from the lesson and invite other students to guess the word.

Guess the punch line
Students tell a joke in English through their avatar, stopping before the punch line. Other students listen to the joke and try to guess the punch line.

Guess who
Students use their avatar to share facts about a famous person or someone known to the class. Other students ask questions (you could set a limit of 20) to find out who the person is.

Why this works ⏵ | **Adding an avatar voice**
Avatars are a great way to add interest to activities which students might otherwise find dull, such as revising vocabulary or listening to instructions. Doing things in a way that captures their imagination can help with wandering attention – something that may particularly affect younger students; and they can use their avatars at different points during the year to give voice to various tasks. For shy or nervous students, using an avatar may lower anxiety and give them more confidence to participate in activities. Recorded instructions give them the additional support of being able to listen to the avatar as often as they want. However, as a note of caution, while using an avatar might help some students overcome initial shyness, you should ensure that they don't become over-reliant on communicating through the avatar. And if the students have created alter-ego avatars, make sure you know which one belongs to which student!

App smashing

App smashing involves combining two or more apps to complete a task or project. We have already encountered some basic examples of app smashing in this book; for example, combining the camera with a collage maker, combining photos with sound or text, and combining photos with a book creator. Similarly, avatars can be combined with other apps to enhance a project; for example, adding an avatar as a presenter to introduce an e-book or a film. App smashing is a way of maximizing the potential of a mobile device, allowing us to mix media types.

Tellagami is a popular avatar app used in app smashing. Widely used in education, it works on both iOS and Android devices as a freemium app (the educational version requires a one-off payment). Unlike those in the Voki for Education app, the avatars (or 'Gamis') in Tellagami are all human, though students can build in variety by selecting from a range of background and clothing options. Students can use their personalized Gamis in a number of ways, from reading out a prepared text through to introducing a project.

In the following app smashing activity, students combine the camera with the Tellagami and Book Creator apps.

VIDEO AND ANIMATION

Try this 👉 **Book introductions**

We can use the Gami to give an introduction to the book that students created in Chapter 4. Put students into the same groups they were in for the book and ask them to take a group photo. They should frame the photo so that it is just off-centre, with space for the Gami to be added later on. Once they are happy with the photo, they open Tellagami, tap on the option for 'background', and import the group photo. Students can now create their Gami and place it to the left or right so that it doesn't obscure the people in the photo. Students type in or voice-record the authors' names and add them to the first page of the book. The Gami will then appear as though it is introducing the students and their work. You can apply this principle to other media types; for example, you could add the Gami to students' films and to some of the activities that we will explore in the following chapters.

Why this works ⏭ **App smashing and the four Cs**

App smashing adds an element of fun to activities, while extending the collaborative challenge for students as they work together on joint projects. Students engage in critical thinking as they choose which apps to use together and tap into their creativity as they shape the content. They also practise a range of language skills as they discuss, write, record, listen, and share.

Animation

While avatars allow us to add animated characters to students' work, we can take animation a step further by creating entirely animated videos. There are a number of apps that allow you to do this. At the time of writing, the best ones are only for iOS mobile devices, but you can look in your app store or see if there's a browser-based version you can use with other devices. For iOS, Sock Puppets and Puppet Pals will particularly appeal to young learners. These apps allow students to create animated scenes to which they can add their own voiceover. Other apps, such as Plotagon, allow you to type in dialogue which automatically transforms into an animated video.

Try this 👉 **Apps for active dialogues**

First, choose a dialogue that you want to focus on. Then, using your chosen app, ask students to work together to decide on characters, setting, and background. Next, they should use the apps to create the scene and then add the dialogue. Depending on the app used, this will involve either voice-recording or typing. Once complete, the animation can be shared with the class.
As a follow up, students can extend the dialogue, for example to say what happens after the extract in the coursebook. Alternatively, they can use the characters from the dialogue as a springboard to create new dialogues and scenes. When the students are comfortable using the app, they can create their own dialogues.

VIDEO AND ANIMATION

Why this works ➡️

> **Making use of video and animation**
>
> Making videos on mobile devices is becoming more and more common. Many students will be comfortable and well practised in doing so, and teachers can use this to their advantage. Students will reflect their own interests through what they choose to record, giving them more autonomy in their learning. Making videos isn't new, but mobile technology has opened up new opportunities for the innovative use of video in the classroom. Making and using videos continues our movement towards the transformative side of the SAMR model.

9 Multimodal approaches and alternative realities

We have seen through the course of this book that mobile learning allows students to conduct research, record and watch videos, and share content. In this chapter, we will consider how mobile devices can be used to enhance or alter reality in ways that has the potential to lead to even more engaging and effective learning.

Augmented reality enables users to interact with virtual content (for example, video, music, text, or images) layered on top of their real-world environment using an app on a mobile device. **Virtual reality** puts users in an entirely virtual world and allows them to interact in it, using a mobile device and a headset. These technologies have the potential to transform the ways you teach, by creating immersive and collaborative environments that both support multimodal input and put the student at the centre of learning. Static images can be made to spring to life, and students will be able to do all manner of things, from creating interactive sticky notes and poster displays to taking a 360° tour of London or shopping in a virtual supermarket. By their very nature, both of these technologies take us over to the transformative side of the SAMR model (see Chapter 2).

Adding links, videos, and text to an image

The ThingLink app, available for iOS and Android, allows students to tag an image with content from anywhere on the internet, adding text and embedding video, audio, or website links. This makes the image interactive, information-rich, and engaging. ThingLink requires you to create an account in order to use it. Once you have signed in, choose a picture from your mobile device. You can add content by tapping anywhere on the picture. It can then be shared by email, turned into a QR code (see Chapter 5), or uploaded to a website.

Try this **All about me: multimodal posters**

This activity can be adapted to any coursebook topic and be done in class or set as homework. Ask students to take selfies with their mobile device and use them on ThingLink to create a multimodal poster like the one in Figure 9.1. They should add tags containing text and YouTube clips to give personal information about themselves. For example:

- a favourite style of music
- a favourite song
- a favourite contemporary group or singer
- an old group or singer that they like.

79

9   MULTIMODAL APPROACHES AND ALTERNATIVE REALITIES

Once they have created their multimodal poster, they should share the link to it via email or upload it to the class website or chat group. Alternatively, you could turn the links into QR codes and print them out to display around the classroom. Once the QR codes are on display, students can walk round and look at their classmates' posters, finding those who have similar musical tastes.

FIGURE 9.1   *Multimodal poster*

✓ **Getting it right**   **Avoiding the explicit**

When dealing with topics such as music, make sure students choose songs which are appropriate for the classroom. Some songs have explicit lyrics or videos, so make clear what is and isn't acceptable.

Why this works ▶   **Practising multimodal skills**

Creating multimodal posters helps to develop students' digital literacy skills, as they are required to work with different media types. Adding video, audio, and links to posters makes for interesting, informative, and impressive results. Students can also share and participate in other people's work more easily. The versatility of such posters means that they are as relevant for content-based language teaching (CBLT) as they are for exam preparation through revision projects.

Try this 👉 **Vocabulary collages**

This activity is best done as a combination of class work and homework. Choose the vocabulary area that you want students to revise. For homework, ask students to take photos which illustrate the vocabulary. In class, students work in small groups to create a collage with the photos using a collage maker app (see Chapter 4). Once they have created the collage, they should upload it to ThingLink. Using the 'add text' option, they can create text tags providing definitions of the vocabulary items in the collage, example sentences, or links to related content online. When they have finished, students should save and share their collages. Students can use the collages to 'test' their vocabulary knowledge by guessing the words that appear in the collage, then clicking on the tags to see if they are correct.

Why this works ▶ **Interactive collages**

Creating interactive vocabulary collages is a useful exercise to help prepare students for end-of-term tests. First, the students actively invest in their revision by taking photos of the topic vocabulary, which in itself requires an understanding of the words. Creating the ThingLink collage revises the spelling of the words (and with a premium ThingLink account, even the pronunciation). Once created, the collage is effectively an exercise with a hidden answer key that students can use to revise the vocabulary. Interactive collages work particularly well as a way of bringing interactivity to wordlists often found in coursebooks. They can also be useful when teaching in content and language integrated learning (CLIL) contexts, as students can create posters and other resources about specific topics.

Augmented reality

You may have heard about augmented reality (AR) from stories in the media and be aware of the popularity of AR games such as Pokemon Go. You may even have seen AR versions of advertisements, for example during the ad breaks for a programme you're watching via a streaming service. In basic terms, AR is the superimposition of digital information on a user's real-world environment. Digital content and information can be added to anything, from printed materials to locations such as tourist sites, shops, or restaurants.

If you live in an urban area, you can experience AR by downloading and opening the Wikitude app, then pointing your mobile device's camera in any direction. Useful information about the area will appear over the image. It might point you in the direction of a restaurant or give you information about a nearby building or landmark.

AR blends the real and the digital to create a hybrid reality. This means that digital information can be tied to a particular object or physical environment. With AR, users look *through* their devices at the real world, creating a 'magic window' effect where information is superimposed on reality. That's not to say that the QR codes we looked at in Chapter 5 are made obsolete by AR;

they are easier to set up and use, and are an established technology. While AR can now be used with students, it is still early days for this technology. There are a number of different providers and platforms, and each upgrade to a platform will alter how it works.

AR apps

We'll start by looking at how we can use simple AR apps in our teaching and move towards creating our own AR activities. For AR to work, you need two things: an AR app and a 'trigger'. You need the app to be able to see augmented content, and the trigger is what makes the augmented content appear. Within reason, a trigger can be any object, though in the classroom they are usually based around images. You point your mobile device at the trigger to activate the augmented content.

A number of educational companies have developed pre-made triggers that you can print out or display on a screen and activate with a mobile device. For example, AR Flashcards produces sets of augmented flashcards for use with young learners. In String (for iOS only), you can trigger dragons and aliens, which act as prompts for storytelling. Quiver (for iOS and Android) provides a number of triggers that you can use in conjunction with pictures you print out from their website and colour in.

Try this **AR animal flashcards**

Use AR Flashcards – Animal Alphabet (for iOS and Android) with young learners to practise speaking and spelling. First, download a set of augmented animal alphabet cards and print them out. Show students that when you point the camera on your mobile device at a letter, an animal appears. When you touch the animal, it says the letter and the name of the animal. Ask students to use their mobile device (or yours, if they are very young) to discover the animals and practise saying the name of the animal by touching and repeating. They can also practise spelling the name of the animal.

Try this **Bring pictures to life**

First print out colouring sheets from the Quiver app and ask students to colour in their pictures for homework. In class, they should open the app and point the camera on their mobile device at the pictures. Students will love seeing their work transformed into 3D images which can move around.

In addition to commercially produced AR activities, there are apps which allow the creation of your own activities, which can augment both coursebook material and students' work.

Blippar

Blippar is a **visual discovery app** that brings the physical world to life through mobile devices. Once you have downloaded the Blippar app (available for iOS and Android), you can scan – or 'blipp' – objects you're interested in to unlock relevant information and content.

Try this **Seeing is believing**

Ask students to download Blippar onto their mobile device. Tell them the app will try to provide information about any object they point their device at.

MULTIMODAL APPROACHES AND ALTERNATIVE REALITIES

Explain that, since the app doesn't recognize everything in the world, it might not always be accurate; as such, the class is going to do some **beta testing**. Before the next lesson, students should use the app on as many different things as possible and make a note of what happens (for example, by taking a screenshot after each blipp). If they point at a fruit, does the app name it correctly? And if they point at their cat, does it identify the right type of animal? In the next class, ask for general feedback, then put students into small groups to discuss what they blipped and how accurate the app was. Bring the class back together and discuss what feedback they would give about the app. Would they recommend it? What improvements would they suggest?

Try this → **Blipp coursebook photos**

Ask students to use Blippar on coursebook photos to identify relevant vocabulary. For example, if they blipp a cityscape, the app might bring up words such as 'travel', 'transport system', or 'industry'. Students should note down the words that the app identifies, then check in pairs which of the suggested words are actually in the photo. Finish the activity by asking students for words that the app correctly identified. Although Blippar is a relatively sophisticated app, be aware that it doesn't usually recognize the actual place in the photo (for example, Manhattan or the Golden Gate Bridge) but uses the general context to identify words relating to it.

Why this works →

> **Blipping vocabulary!**
>
> As a different way of introducing vocabulary, Blippar increases students' motivation to find out what words mean. For this reason, they will probably want to use the app outside class, which means they will be doing more reading and vocabulary work independently.

At the time of writing, Blippar is still developing its platforms and materials, so many teachers use another more established app, Aurasma, to create their AR activities.

Aurasma

Aurasma is available as a free app for iOS and Android mobile devices. Its image-recognition technology uses a mobile device's camera to recognize objects in the real world and then overlays information on top of them, such as videos, animations, and links to web pages. Aurasma calls its augmented content an 'aura'. It adds content to a channel which users must follow to view the aura. Creating an aura needs a trigger and an overlay, which you scan and activate with a mobile device.

Try this → **Adding a model answer**

This activity works well for exam preparation classes. Before the lesson, find a suitable speaking task in your coursebook. Open the camera on your mobile device and record a short video of yourself giving a 'model' answer to the speaking task. Save the recording on your device. Open Aurasma and tap on the '+' button. Next, take a photo of the speaking task and when prompted for the 'overlay', choose your video recording. Follow the instructions in the app to create and save your aura. Students do the speaking task in class, but share the aura link with them afterwards so that they can compare their answer to your model answer in their own time.

MULTIMODAL APPROACHES AND ALTERNATIVE REALITIES

✓ Getting it right

Making an aura

There are two ways to make an aura. The quickest way is in the app itself, although this limits what you can create and how. You can also use a computer to access Aurasma Studio, an online platform for creating auras which allows for the use of a wider selection of media and the addition of URLs. You need to create an account, but it is free to use and there are clear step-by-step directions and instructional videos on how to use the platform.

Why this works ▶

Independent learning

Auras help students to become more independent learners. They reduce students' reliance on the teacher and allow them to work at their own pace. By adding several actions to the same aura, students are able to decide which activities they want or feel they need to do. For example, in grammar handouts you could use one action to take confident students to a video, while those who need more help could go to a website with further activities. Moreover, creating auras adds extra re-usable tasks to your coursebook material. Tasks might include model texts, answers, extensive reading or listening, or differentiated practice activities for mixed-ability classes.

Try this ☞

Augmented book reviews

This activity works well with graded readers. When students have finished reading their book, get them to video-record themselves reviewing it. First, discuss what they should include in the review:

- an overview of the plot
- an overview of the character
- what they liked
- what they disliked
- their recommendation.

Then ask students to discuss their book in pairs, addressing these points and making notes for their review. After practising their reviews in pairs, ask students to use their mobile device to record them. Next, students choose the book's front cover as the trigger in Aurasma and add their recorded video review as the overlay. They then create the aura and share the link. Their reviews will appear whenever a student scans the book's front cover.

✓ Getting it right

Using Aurasma for differentiation

As noted above, there are two ways to make an aura. Using the Aurasma Studio platform allows you to make more interactive auras. At the 'add an overlay' stage, there is the option to 'add actions'. This allows you to, for example, add links to websites. Making use of these functions allows us to create different learning paths for our students.

MULTIMODAL APPROACHES AND ALTERNATIVE REALITIES

Why this works ▶ **Video reviews**

While students might regard writing book reviews as dull language practice, outside class they are likely to read online reviews of music, video games, or films, and perhaps even post their own reviews. Using auras brings the task of reviewing closer to real life, as students can attach their opinions to book covers, film posters, DVD cases, etc.

Try this ☞ **Augmented handouts**

Next time you create your own handout, give it an aura so students can access extra content. Create the handout as you usually would and copy it. On the second copy, complete the exercise with the correct answers. Decide what the extra content is going to be, such as a link to an online video or an audio file, and copy the URLs. Now go to Aurasma. Identify your original handout as the trigger and the completed handout as the overlay. Then use 'add action' to add the URLs, and save the aura on your channel.

Before the lesson, put extra copies of the handout around the room and give each student their own copy of the handout to complete. When they have finished, they should go to one of the clean copies around the room and scan it to reveal the answer key. By tapping on their screen, they will be taken to the next piece of content. It is best to do this on a flat surface so that students can hover their device over the handout to see the answers and simultaneously note down any corrections. You might want to make the students aware that if they are using the app for the first time, it may take a few attempts to activate the aura. This will improve with practice.

Virtual reality

As we have seen, AR places a layer on the real world. Virtual reality (VR), or virtual realities, differs from AR in that it involves immersing yourself in a completely different world. VR is a computer technology that creates an environment, fictitious or mirroring the real world, which users can enter and interact with as though it were real. VR can also create sensory experiences involving touch, hearing, sight, and smell. It allows students to interact in life-like environments which they might not be able to experience otherwise, and without the time and expense involved in actually going there. Students can learn directly through a simulated experience and get instant feedback on their performance.

Now that affordable viewing systems are available, VR is no longer a distant dream in terms of being an effective tool in the classroom – although these systems do still require relatively high-end mobile devices to power them. To view AR, all we need is a camera and an app, but for VR we need additional tools in order to immerse ourselves in the virtual world. One way to do this is by using a headset such as an Oculus Rift (Figure 9.2), but Google has developed a more affordable alternative, Google Cardboard (Figure 9.3), which has helped to popularize the use of VR in the classroom.

FIGURE 9.2   *Oculus Rift*

FIGURE 9.3   *Google Cardboard*

Google Cardboard is a viewing system for smartphones (though note that it is geared towards Android; there is less software available for iOS). To enter the VR world, put your phone inside the viewing system, hold the lenses over your eyes, and put on a pair of headphones.

Thanks to the affordability of Google Cardboard, VR is beginning to have an impact on education, with students now able to 'enter' the human body, visit the surface of Mars, or use Google Expeditions to explore different countries. In language teaching, it may still be some time before we ask students to put on headsets and interact with virtual teachers. But for now, a relatively accessible option is to immerse yourself in a 360° video representation of the world.

360° videos

360° videos are shot from every angle so that there are no breaks when you look up or down, or from side to side. And unlike traditional video, which plays from start to finish in a fixed manner, you can manipulate the 360° video to change the view. You can view 360° videos on most browsers or through 360° video apps, but the viewing experience is much more

MULTIMODAL APPROACHES AND ALTERNATIVE REALITIES

immersive when you use a VR headset. There is an increasingly large choice of 360° videos that can help to bring a coursebook topic to life. You can find good examples on YouTube, Google Street View, and Facebook; and ThingLink has a separate app for them. It's like adding virtual elements of a field trip to a lesson, where instead of simply reading or talking about the topic, students can actually be immersed in the visual environment.

Try this — **From London tours to rollercoasters**

Before the lesson, find a 360° video that fits your coursebook topic and decide how best to share it with students (as a link, a QR code, etc.). If you have enough Google Cardboard headsets and the equivalent number of suitably high-end smartphones, put students in pairs, with one wearing the headset. This student watches the video and describes what they see, while their partner makes notes. Ask students to swap roles halfway through. Students discuss their notes, comparing their accuracy with what they saw. Then ask the whole class to discuss the experience. For example, for a tour of London, ask about the different places; for a rollercoaster video, elicit adjectives to describe how they felt.

✓ Getting it right — **No headsets**

Having headsets allows for a more immersive experience, but the same activity can still work without them. If the activity centres around a YouTube 360° video, for example, you can specify how you are watching the video so that it changes to work with a VR headset or without. When working in pairs, Student A could simply view the video directly in a browser on their mobile device, making sure the screen is not visible to Student B.

Why this works — **An immersive experience**

In SAMR terms, both AR and VR are transformative technologies which have the potential to modify our classroom practice. By allowing us to add layers of digital information to the objects around us, we can create an interactive learning experience that can truly engage students. Using the platforms and apps described in this chapter, we can link language to real-world environments. By layering support and guidance within our AR creations, we are modifying the ways in which our students engage in classroom language learning, allowing students to take control over their learning and discover things for themselves, while at the same time providing a rich context for language practice. People often refer to AR as a way of bringing learning to life, a phrase that is even more applicable to VR, which creates fully immersive environments. While it is still no substitute for a real environment, VR has the potential to create places and scenarios in which our students can practise authentic language. Even now, still in its infancy, VR can give students the sense of visiting places and experiencing activities that have previously only been images on a screen or pictures in a book.

10 Tools for the teacher

In this final chapter, we look at mobile device tools that make life easier for teachers. With apps and access to the internet, the possibilities are endless: you are able to access or share documents and take the class register on your mobile device; you can use apps to help with seating arrangements and grouping students; there are even apps for digitizing your classroom reward systems. A quick internet search will locate apps for these, but in this chapter we'll focus on using tools for offering differentiated learning and ensuring that all students understand the lesson content. Being able to assess students' understanding on an individual, lesson-by-lesson basis means we can adjust lessons more easily to meet their various needs.

In large classes, it is often hard to know exactly how each student is doing until they take a test. It can also be difficult to work with students individually. A lot of teaching is done in what we call 'lockstep', where the students follow the pace set by the teacher. In such contexts, if students don't understand a language presentation, they are likely to fall behind and lose motivation. One way to address this is by creating short recordings of things such as language presentations or help videos, which you can then share with students to watch outside class if necessary to help them keep up. Bite-sized screen recordings can be paused and repeated, allowing students to easily watch them whenever they need to. They are helpful when students haven't understood your class presentation, were absent from the lesson, or if you weren't on hand to help.

Screen recording

Screen recording (also referred to as 'screen capture' or 'screen casting') is the term for capturing content on the screen of your mobile device. The easiest way to make a video of a language presentation is by using a whiteboard app on your mobile device, as we shall see later in the chapter. Although it is slightly more complicated, recording the screen of your device can also be done via a computer.

Making a video of what you are doing on your mobile device isn't as straightforward as it sounds, because if you use an iOS or Windows device, there is no app that does it for you. The easiest way to do it is by projecting your mobile device through a computer (see Chapter 1). If you use a Mac computer, you can use QuickTime to record the projected screen. Alternatively, you can record the projection using a website such as Screencast-O-Matic. For Android apps, go to the app store and search

TOOLS FOR THE TEACHER

for 'screen recorder'. To help you get started, YouTube has many tutorials explaining how to record with your chosen screen recording app.

If there is a particular app you want your students to use, you can save class time by creating a video tutorial explaining how to use it. Preparation is very important, so leave the actual recording until you have planned the tutorial carefully.

Try this — **Create a video tutorial for an app**

Open the app and make a note of the steps you need to follow to use it. For example, for the Voki for Education app (see Chapter 8) the steps are:
- open the app and tap on the 'head' symbol in the top left-hand corner
- choose a character from the menu
- choose the clothes for the character (and so on)
- when the avatar is ready, tap on the 'record' symbol and add audio
- tap on the 'share' button in the bottom right-hand corner
- share the avatar.

Once you have noted the relevant steps, plan your tutorial. Restart the app and rehearse what you will say and do at each stage before you record. When you are ready, press 'record' and talk through the process. You can always delete the recording and do it again until you are satisfied with it. Save your recording and share it with your students to watch when they need to.

Using a whiteboard app

As the name suggests, a whiteboard app turns the screen of a mobile device into a whiteboard space. This is particularly useful when we want to combine screen recording with language instruction. Most whiteboard apps come with the ability to record what is on the screen, and with some you can also upload media such as photos and presentation slides. This makes whiteboard apps ideal for recording presentations, task instructions, examples, and so on. As with the screen recordings we looked at previously, they can be useful for providing step-by-step explanations, for example to explain grammar. Students can watch, pause, and replay recordings until they understand the content. Alternatively, you could ask students to produce their own recordings to demonstrate their understanding of particular grammar points or vocabulary.

There are a number of apps available for different devices. You have to pay for many of them, and they vary in complexity. Some, for example, create a simple screen recording with a link to it online that you can send to students, while others allow you to create user accounts and store your recordings on the device itself. To see what's available, search for 'whiteboard' in your app store. A popular app is Explain Everything (compatible with all devices, although you have to pay for it).

✓ Getting it right **Screen size and styluses**

Though whiteboard apps are available for all types of mobile device, if your students are using smartphones, they may find that the smaller size of the screen makes it harder to manipulate whiteboard content. Using a stylus (a pen-like tool for touchscreen mobile devices) would help to overcome this.

Try this 👉 **Recording a grammar presentation**

Think about how you would usually help students to understand a particular grammar point and order your ideas in a logical sequence. For example:
- examples to provide context
- questions to elicit form and meaning
- display form
- timeline (where necessary)
- check understanding.

Consider what you will say/put on the whiteboard at each stage. Open the whiteboard app and create a title page on the first slide. Use a new slide for each step in the presentation. After rehearsing, record and save your presentation. Teach your lesson as usual and make the video available to students for later reference.

✓ **Getting it right** | **Keep it short**

Make sure recordings aren't too long; experienced 'screencasters' recommend a five- to ten-minute limit. If necessary, treat the recording as a recap and cover only the essential parts of the presentation.

Why this works ➡ **Use it again and again**

Screen recording presentations will add to your preparation time. However, making decisions about what to include or leave out can make your classroom presentation more effective, and you can reuse the screen recording whenever you teach the language point.

Flipped learning

A typical language presentation involves the teacher presenting a point in class, with students listening then doing practice activities, followed by more for homework. While there is nothing wrong with this teacher-centred approach, some teachers have started to 'flip' their classrooms so that students engage with the input at home using their mobile devices and spend class time on practice.

Mobile device use in class isn't solely responsible for the effectiveness of flipped learning, but it has contributed significantly to its uptake. Since videos can be created, viewed, and shared via simple recording apps on mobile devices, a number of barriers around accessibility have been removed. This is not to claim that flipped learning is without issues. As a relatively new development in education, more research is needed to establish the advantages and disadvantages. In the meantime, experiment and see whether aspects of flipped learning work for you and your students.

Try this 👉 **Videoed flashcards**

Prior to a vocabulary lesson using flashcards, take a photo of each card to present on separate whiteboard slides. On each slide, write the word shown.

Create another set of slides with the same flashcards, but this time write clues for the word; for example, give the first letter. Then use the whiteboard app to create a vocabulary presentation. For the first set of flashcards, say the word as you record. After the first set, give an instruction such as *Can you remember the words?* As you record the second set, do not say anything, as students will need to guess what the words are. Share the presentation with students to view at home, and in the next lesson use the real flashcards to check their knowledge. If you teach young learners, you could ask them to create their own flashcards for the words you want to review, either by taking photos themselves or drawing pictures for you to photograph.

✓ Getting it right

Student cooperation

Not all students will necessarily cooperate with flipped learning. Some may not watch a video set for homework, for example. One way to deal with this is to do what was intended in class with those who have watched the video and to get those who haven't to watch it separately, then join the class activity.

Why this works ⏵

Active learning

Being able to watch instructional videos in their own time gives students more flexibility, as they can watch them as often as they like, repeat certain sections, etc. With flipped learning, class time is arguably more actively (and therefore more profitably) spent working on students' understanding and communication – through, for example, student-led project work, practice activities, and discussions.

Mobile devices and informal assessment

Mobile devices are useful tools for assessing students' work; in fact, some of the projects explored in this book could be used to informally assess student learning, giving teachers and students valuable ongoing feedback. Most assessment of students tends to be done formally, for example through mid-year and end-of-year testing. While this kind of summative testing will always have a place in language teaching, more informal, formative feedback from projects and quizzes, etc. can allow us to monitor learning more frequently, making it possible to continually adjust our teaching to meet students' needs.

Quizzes

Using quizzes in class is a great way to obtain continuous feedback on students' learning. You can create quizzes on a wide range of websites and apps, then give students a code to access the quiz on their mobile devices. Since these apps work on any device, this kind of informal assessment works equally well in BYOD classrooms and ones using school-owned devices. Look for websites or apps that allow you to create an account where you can store your quizzes, include a dashboard so you can see how students are doing, and provide tutorials, which are also a useful feature. Three popular examples are Kahoot!, Formative, and Socrative.

Kahoot! is a web-based learning platform which can be used to make quizzes, polls, or discussions, all of which can contain images and video. Once you have created a quiz, direct students to the site and give them the code so they can access it. Note that you will need to display the quiz via a shared screen, as students can only use their mobile device to answer questions, not see the questions themselves; this is because Kahoot! is intended to be used in group settings, with the shared screen maintaining group cohesion. Also note that the quiz doesn't give detailed feedback on performance, only the number of questions students get right or wrong.

Formative is another web-based platform which works in a similar way to Kahoot! but provides a wider range of quiz options. Unlike Kahoot!, where mobile devices are only used to answer questions, the questions also appear on students' screens. The 'live results' screen shows all students' answers, so you can see exactly who got what right and wrong.

Socrative works both through a browser and two apps – one for creating the quiz and one for taking it. Socrative allows you to make short quizzes (for example, multiple-choice, true/false) and has an excellent dashboard showing students' performance throughout the quiz.

Try this **Adapt an exercise**

Rather than writing your own questions, try adapting workbook or coursebook exercises. Type the questions into one of the online quiz makers mentioned above and save your quiz so you can access it whenever you wish. You can also link it to the screen recordings we explored earlier in this chapter to 'target' students who are likely to benefit from going through a topic again.

Why this works **Using quizzes**

Repurposing exercises to complete on mobile devices as quiz games can give students a welcome change from standard class work. They can be taken at home as often as students wish, saving class time for more communicative activities. Students can check their answers immediately, and instant feedback on their performance is provided via the dashboard. This feedback can be used by both you and your students to review progress over time.

Exit tickets

If you have used Kahoot!, Formative, or Socrative to make a quiz, you will have noticed the function called 'exit ticket'. This is another type of assessment tool that gives teachers a way to informally assess how well students have understood a lesson. Exit tickets provide a useful alternative to quizzes, as they tend to be shorter and often only need a quick answer.

TOOLS FOR THE TEACHER

A good exit ticket has no more than five questions that students can complete quickly at the end of class. The questions should focus on the objective of the lesson and the skill or language point covered; for example, 'name one thing you learned in today's lesson' or, for lower levels and younger students, 'tell me three words we learned today'.

✓ **Getting it right** | **Introducing exit tickets to your class**
For exit tickets to work effectively, students need to take them seriously. Suddenly introducing them might come as too much of a surprise, so tell students ahead of time that you are going to trial them for a certain amount of time to see how well they work. Review them after this period is over, and make sure to ask students for their opinions, too.

Try this **Emoji exit tickets**

Towards the end of a lesson, draw four emoji representing a happy face, a sad face, a confused face, and a face with a neutral expression on the board. Elicit what emotions are expressed by the faces. Ask the students to send you a text or an instant message on their mobile device that answers the question: 'How do you feel about today's lesson?' Tell them to send you one of the four emoji on the board as their response. You could also ask them to add a short sentence explaining why they chose that particular emoji. Look at the responses to gauge students' feelings about the lesson. A lot of 'confused' faces probably indicates that you need to review the lesson. One or two confused faces will identify which students you might need to follow up with individually.

Try this **QR exit tickets**

Creating a QR code for an exit ticket is a way of making exit tickets part of daily classroom procedure. By placing the QR code near the door of the classroom, students can be prompted to scan it as they leave class. Before introducing it, you will need to create an exit ticket survey. Google Forms is a good option, as it has the added advantage of collating the results for you. Create a survey with these three questions:

1 What did you learn in class today?
2 How did you feel about today's lesson?
3 Is there anything you didn't understand today?

Once you have created the survey, copy the URL link and create the QR code, then print it out as a classroom poster (see Chapter 5). At the end of each lesson, remind students to scan the QR code and complete the exit ticket survey. Once they have completed the survey, look through their responses to determine how well they have understood the lesson.

Try this **Three words**

Towards the end of a vocabulary lesson, ask students to make a note of three (or more) words they learned. For homework, they should create a short video that includes the three new words. They could simply write each new word with its definition on a piece of paper and capture it on video, but encourage them to be more creative, as this will help to deepen their understanding.

Students should share their video with the class so that you can check it and their peers can comment if they wish. This activity can be done using one of the many apps we have looked at in this book, such as the Book Creator app (see Chapter 4) or a whiteboard app (see page 89).

Why this works ▶

> **A chance to reflect**
>
> As with quizzes, exit tickets give students a chance to reflect and comment on their learning. They can give their feedback anonymously and are therefore less likely to feel embarrassed if they struggled with something. For teachers, exit tickets provide a snapshot of how students felt about a particular lesson, allowing for more effective planning of future lessons.

Using digital coursebooks

Once you and your students have become accustomed to mobile device use in your classroom, you might want to consider moving from using a paper-based to a digital coursebook. Most digital coursebooks are not that dissimilar to their paper versions. One obvious difference is that you tap or swipe between pages instead of physically turning them. Another difference is that you can easily enlarge a picture or text in a digital coursebook. This is great if you want students to look at a picture in more detail, or if you have students with visual impairments who require larger type. Some digital coursebooks will let students add notes and links to other resources such as a dictionary. You can introduce some of these features so that students understand their purpose and feel confident using them.

Try this ☞ **How does it work?**

Before class, open the digital coursebook on your device and make a note of some of the interactive features it has and how they are used (jumping to a page, making text notes, using a pen tool, enlarging a photo, accessing audio, voice recording, etc.). On the board, write a list of the features you want to highlight. Put students into small groups to identify these features. When you're ready to check answers, display the book on your device and ask students to name the tools (if you are projecting onto a whiteboard, you can write the name of the feature next to it).

Digital coursebooks contain all the audio files, which means that instead of playing the audio yourself, students can use their headphones and listen at their own pace. This can reduce pressure on students and make listening activities feel less like a test. Digital coursebooks also make it easy for students to listen and read at the same time. This will appeal to students who don't find reading easy and to those for whom listening is a struggle – and also to those who simply enjoy doing both at the same time!

Why this works ▶ **The benefits of digital coursebooks**

When using a digital coursebook in the classroom, little else should need to change; you can still manage the class in the same way and decide whether or not to use the digital coursebook just as you would use a printed one. But one obvious advantage of using a digital coursebook is that there is less to carry around. Students will be able to use their mobile device to access the coursebook, workbook, and other resources such as a class reader or dictionary.

A second advantage is that the features of a digital coursebook will appeal to different types of learner, from those that like to engage with media such as audio and video to those who prefer the traditional coursebook format. This can only serve to enrich the learning experience and present more learning opportunities for a greater number of students.

Besides using published e-books, it is easy for teachers to create their own e-material. For example, the Book Creator app (see Chapter 4) could be used to create up-to-date material that addresses your students' specific needs and complements the core course material.

As with many of the tools and activities we have explored in this book, digital coursebooks help us to find new ways of working in the classroom and give us new opportunities to improve our students' language learning.

Glossary

Adaptor A device for connecting pieces of electrical equipment that were not designed to fit together.

Airplane mode A setting on mobile devices that prevents the device from accessing a phone or wi-fi network.

App (applications) Software designed to run on mobile devices and computers. Apps may be pre-installed on a particular device or downloaded from the app store.

App smashing The process of using multiple apps to create projects or complete tasks.

App store A distribution platform for purchasing and downloading apps onto computers and mobile devices. For Apple, this will be the iOS app store; for Android, it will be sites such as Google Play or Amazon; and for Windows, it will be the Microsoft Store.

Augmented reality A technology that combines computer-generated content on a screen with the real object or scene that you are looking at.

Avatar A graphic image of a person or an animal that represents a user on a computer, especially in a computer game or online.

Beta testing The term for testing an app or software under real-life conditions.

Browser A program that lets you look at or read documents on the world wide web.

Chat group A group of people who communicate regularly via the internet by means of messaging apps.

Closed group A specific group of people who use the same social networking space to share information. The group can only be accessed by certain people, unlike an open group that anyone can join.

Cross-platform A program or device that can be used with different types of device or program.

Data package (or data plan) A service offered by mobile phone companies that allows users to access the internet via 3G or 4G for a monthly cost.

Digital footprint The information about a particular person that exists on the internet as a result of their online activities.

Digital literacy The knowledge and skills needed to effectively use mobile devices. This includes the ability to locate, organize, understand, evaluate, and analyse information found when using the device on a network.

Dongle A small device that is used with a computer, especially to access protected software or the internet.

Emoji Small digital images used in electronic messages and online to express an idea, emotion, object, etc.

Emoticon Small digital representations of ideas and emotions, created using keyboard characters.

Freemium A business model whereby a basic version of a product or service is provided free of charge, with the option to pay for 'premium' features.

Hardware The physical parts that constitute a mobile device or computer.

HDMI (High-Definition Multimedia Interface) A system for connecting audio and video devices to electronic equipment such as a television or computer, via a cable.

MP3 A type of audio file. It is a common way to save and store audio.

Podcast A digital audio file that can be taken from the internet and played on a computer or a mobile device.

QR code (Quick Response code) A pattern of black and white squares that contains information, often a web address, that can be read using the camera of a mobile device and a QR reader.

QR creator An app or website where the user can make their own QR codes.

QR reader An app that can scan and decode the information in a QR code.

SAMR (Substitution, Augmentation, Modification, Redefinition) A model designed to help educators consider the effects of technology on learning.

Selfie A photo of oneself, typically taken on a mobile device or webcam and shared via social media.

Smartphone A mobile phone that also has some of the functions of a computer; for example, the facility to use apps and access the internet.

97

GLOSSARY

Social network A site or application through which users can communicate with each other by sharing information, messages, images, etc.

Software The operating system and programs used on a computer or mobile device.

Tablet (or tablet computer) A touchscreen multimedia device – typically smaller than a laptop but larger than a phone – which can be used, for example, to play videos, read e-books, and access the internet.

Tag A word or phrase with the symbol '#' in front of it, included in some messages sent on social networks so that you can search for all messages with the same tag.

URL (Uniform Resource Locator) Typically, the address of a web page.

VGA (Video Graphics Array) A connector that joins video devices such as a computer to a projector.

Virtual reality An immersive environment created by a computer that seems almost real to the user, who can interact with the environment using compatible equipment.

Visual discovery app An app which uses image recognition and augmented reality to give additional information about the real world.

Useful apps and websites

Further support for using mobile devices in the classroom

The OUP ELT Blog publishes regular articles for teachers. Search for 'Tablets and apps in your school' and 'How to bluff your way through the changes affecting English language teaching'.
https://oupeltglobalblog.com

OUP ELT also broadcasts regular webinars for teachers. Create a free account in order to access the webinar library, which is organized by topic. Select 'Technology' and look for 'Digitalising your pencil case', 'Going mobile: choices and challenges', 'Online risk and safety for language learners and teachers', and others.
https://elt.oup.com/feature/global/webinars

The British Council posts useful articles on its Teaching English website. Search for 'Mobile pedagogy for English language teaching'.
www.teachingenglish.org.uk

The British Council also broadcasts regular webinars and seminars for ELT professionals. For example, search for 'A beginner's guide to mobile learning in ELT'.
https://englishagenda.britishcouncil.org/events

The P21 Partnership for 21st Century Learning website provides a framework for 21st century skills, including digital literacy skills.
www.p21.org

Ruben Puentedura's blog discusses applying the SAMR model to education.
http://hippasus.com/blog

The Webwise website has helpful advice on using technology in education, including examples of acceptable use policies and approaches to online safety.
www.webwise.ie

The Bullying UK website offers advice on dealing with cyberbullying and staying safe online.
www.bullying.co.uk/cyberbullying

Storing and sharing work

Dropbox
www.dropbox.com

iCloud
www.icloud.com

OneDrive
https://onedrive.live.com

Showbie
www.showbie.com

Schoology
www.schoology.com

Facebook
https://www.facebook.com

Edmodo
www.edmodo.com

Social media apps and websites

WhatsApp
www.whatsapp.com

Kik
www.kik.com

Facebook Messenger
https://www.messenger.com

Viber
www.viber.com

Twitter
https://twitter.com

Instagram
www.instagram.com

Snapchat
www.snapchat.com

USEFUL APPS AND WEBSITES

Mirroring

Droid@Screen
http://droid-at-screen.org

X-Mirage
http://x-mirage.com/x-mirage

Text messaging

Examples of txtstories
www.txtlit.co.uk

A dictionary of text language
http://www.webopedia.com/quick_ref/textmessageabbreviations.asp

Emoji

An encyclopedia of emoji
http://emojipedia.org

Copy and paste emoji
http://getemoji.com

Emoji tracker
www.emojitracker.com

Using and sharing photos

Flick
http://getflick.io

Chirp
www.chirp.io

Book Creator
http://bookcreator.com

QR codes

QR Code Generator Pro
www.qr-code-generator.com

QR Stuff
www.qrstuff.com

ClassTools
http://classtools.net/QR

Polls and quizzes

Mentimeter
www.mentimeter.com

Poll Everywhere
www.polleverywhere.com

Google Forms
www.google.com/forms/about

Kahoot!
https://getkahoot.com

Formative
https://goformative.com

Socrative
www.socrative.com

Online noticeboards

Padlet
https://padlet.com

Lino
http://en.linoit.com

Audio recording

AudioBoom
https://audioboom.com

Spreaker
www.spreaker.com

Podcasting

Stitcher
www.stitcher.com

PodOmatic
http://podomatic.com

bossjock studio
http://bossjockstudio.com

GarageBand
www.apple.com/mac/garageband

iTunes
www.apple.com/itunes

Digital storytelling

Educational uses of digital storytelling
https://digitalstorytelling.coe.uh.edu

Adobe Spark
https://spark.adobe.com/about/video

USEFUL APPS AND WEBSITES

PhotoVoice
https://play.google.com/store/apps/details?id=com.photovoice&hl=en_GB

Story Cubes
www.storycubes.com/app

Story Dice
http://thinkamingo.com/story-dice

Story Wheel
https://itunes.apple.com/app/story-wheel/id437068725?mt=8

Rubrics

Digital storytelling: evaluation methods
http://courseweb.ischool.illinois.edu/~jevogel2/lis506/evaluation.html

Kathy Schrock's Guide to Everything: assessment and rubrics
www.schrockguide.net/assessment-and-rubrics.html

Video editing

Well Done U short film competition
www.bbc.co.uk/programmes/p02sx40j

iMovie
www.apple.com/imovie

Splice
https://spliceapp.com

Quik
https://quik.gopro.com/en

Magisto
www.magisto.com

VideoShow
www.videoshowapp.com

Movie Maker
www.microsoft.com/en-gb/store/p/movie-maker-free-video-editor/9nblggh4wwjr

Avatars

Voki for Education
www.voki.com/site/app

Tellagami
https://tellagami.com

WeeMee Avatar Creator
www.weeworld.com/about

Animation

Plotagon
https://plotagon.com

Sock Puppets
http://my.smithmicro.com/sock-puppets-description.html

Puppet Pals
https://itunes.apple.com/app/puppet-pals-hd/id342076546?mt=8

Multimodal approaches and alternative realities

Pokemon Go
www.pokemongo.com

ThingLink
www.thinglink.com/app

Wikitude
www.wikitude.com

Blippar
https://blippar.com/en/solutions/blippar-for-education

Aurasma
https://studio.aurasma.com/landing

AR Flashchards
http://arflashcards.com

String
http://geteducreative.weebly.com/string.html

Quiver
www.quivervision.com/app

Google Expeditions
https://edu.google.com/expeditions

Google Street View
www.google.com/streetview

360° videos on YouTube
www.youtube.com/channel/UCzuqhhs6NWbgTzMuM09WKDQ

360° videos on ThingLink
http://demo.thinglink.com/vr-edu

Screen recording

QuickTime
https://support.apple.com/downloads/quicktime

Screencast-O-Matic
https://screencast-o-matic.com

Explain Everything
https://explaineverything.com

Flipped learning

A flipped learning community
http://flippedlearning.org

How to flip your classroom
http://flippedinstitute.org/how-to-flip